PARTNERING FOR COVID-19 RESPONSE AND RECOVERY

THE ASIAN DEVELOPMENT BANK'S SUPPORT TO INDIA

NOVEMBER 2023

ADB

ASIAN DEVELOPMENT BANK

Notes:
1. In this publication, "$" refers to United States dollars.
2. Project Lead: Rajesh Kumar Deol, Asian Development Bank.
3. Consultants: Sudipto Patra, Kevin Michael Donahue.

On the cover:
• Cover photos courtesy Asian Development Bank.

Other photos:
• ID 217950057© Manoej Paateel | Dreamstime.com | Mumbai, 17 May, 2020 | Closed shops in a Sutar chawl, Kalbadevi during a nationwide lockdown.
• ID 186653558 © Manoej Paateel | Dreamstime.com| A medical officer attends to residents at a COVID-19 coronavirus testing drive during a nationwide lockdown.
• ID 181515889 © Sanjoy Karmakar | Dreamstime.com | Burdwan Town, Purba Bardhaman District, West Bengal / India , 2 May 2020 | People in a queue to collect food grains at a ration shop in Burdwan town during the lock down period due to Novel Coronavirus COVID-19 outbreak.
• Rest of the photographs included in the publication are courtesy Asian Development Bank unless otherwise mentioned.

Contents

Tables, Figures, and Boxes

Foreword

Looking back, the prolonged coronavirus disease (COVID-19) pandemic was nothing short of tumultuous for hundreds of millions of people across the globe battling successive waves of the virus. The rampant spread of COVID-19 forced governments to adopt drastic measures to ensure the health and safety of the population. Poor and vulnerable groups were especially hard hit as health directives forced the closure of businesses and industries, impacting the livelihoods of millions. For India, with its large population and vast geography, the outcomes were exceptionally severe.

In those grim times, India's healthcare and frontline workers worked tirelessly to treat patients, unmindful of the danger. Many inspiring stories of human fortitude amid adversity stood out during the chaos of the pandemic. There were also noteworthy examples of inspiring leadership across the country as the Government of India responded promptly to each phase of the pandemic in a manner that was both proactive and commendable.

The unprecedented health crisis called for prompt actions beyond the business-as-usual approach on the part of multilateral institutions including the Asian Development Bank (ADB). As India's long-standing development partner, ADB worked closely with the government to help deal with the immediate and long-term impacts of the pandemic. Initial ADB assistance was geared to help the government ramp up health system interventions to save lives, inject economic stimulus to secure livelihoods, and strengthen social protection measures.

As India charted its course toward recovery, ADB also provided support for building India's long-term resilience and improving its preparedness for future shocks. To ensure a swift response, ADB fast-tracked its internal business processes and introduced innovative financing instruments in its comprehensive pandemic response strategy.

This report intends to present such interventions as part of ADB's holistic support to India's pandemic response and subsequent recovery effort. This comprehensive documentation explains how ADB's flexible financing modalities—across sovereign and nonsovereign operations, grants, and technical assistance—aided in the country's battle against COVID-19.

I commend our India Resident Mission team for delivering this report that will not only serve as a chronicle of initiatives jointly undertaken by ADB and the Government of India to deal with an unprecedented health emergency but also as a compendium of lessons learned to strengthen the response to any future pandemic.

We remain grateful for the trust the Government of India placed in us, which helped achieve many positive results in ADB-supported initiatives during the pandemic and beyond.

K. Yokoyama

Kenichi Yokoyama, Director General
South Asia Department, Asian Development Bank, Manila

Acknowledgments

This report chronicles the Asian Development Bank's swift and comprehensive support to India's COVID-19 pandemic response and recovery initiatives. It draws from various ADB reports and documents along with field studies to record the testimonials of beneficiaries.

Senior Communications Officer Rajesh Kumar Deol of the India Resident Mission led the preparation of the publication under the guidance of Country Director Takeo Konishi.

ADB consultants Sudipto Patra and Kevin Michael Donahue provided extensive support in compiling and reviewing the report. India Resident Mission Deputy Country Director Hoe Yun Jeong and other ADB staff— including Sonali Khetrapal, Kanupriya Gupta, Madhusudan Patiraj Yadav, Shivendra Sharma, Sanjay Divakar Joshi, Soumya Chattopadhyay, and Asako Maruyama—also thoroughly reviewed key sections and provided valuable inputs to this publication.

Abbreviations

AMRUT	Atal Mission for Rejuvenation and Urban Transformation
ASU	Assam Skill University
CARES	COVID-19 Active Response and Expenditure Support
COVID-19	coronavirus disease
CPRO	COVID-19 Pandemic Response Option
CPS	country partnership strategy
CVC	COVID-19 vaccination center
DMC	developing member country
FPS	fair price shop
GDP	gross domestic product
GESI	gender equity and social inclusion
GVC	global value chain
HWC	health and wellness center
LPG	liquefied petroleum gas
MOHFW	Ministry of Health and Family Welfare
MRCIP	Maharashtra Rural Connectivity Improvement Project
MTS	mass thermal screening
NCD	noncommunicable disease
NGO	nongovernment organization
NICDC	National Industrial Corridor Development Corporation
NICDP	National Industrial Corridor Development Program
ONORC	One Nation One Ration Card
PDS	public distribution system
PM-ABHIM	Pradhan Mantri Ayushman Bharat Health Infrastructure Mission
PMGKY	Pradhan Mantri Garib Kalyan Yojana
PMUY	Pradhan Mantri Ujjwala Yojana
PRC	(the) People's Republic of China
RCCE	Risk Communication and Community Engagement
SPV	special purpose vehicle
TA	technical assistance
TVET	technical and vocational education and training
ULB	urban local body
UNICEF	United Nations Children's Fund
UPHC	urban primary health center

Executive Summary

The Asian Development Bank (ADB) has been a long-standing partner of the Government of India. This report documents ADB's contributions in swiftly providing comprehensive support to India's COVID-19 pandemic response and recovery initiatives. The pandemic hit India in three waves between 2020 and 2022 and had an adverse socioeconomic impact, particularly on the poor and vulnerable population. India, which has huge socio-cultural-geographical diversity, nevertheless overcame numerous challenges, including technical, operational, social, and epidemiological bottlenecks in combating the pandemic. ADB stepped up to partner with the Government of India in its strategic, multisectoral, and well-planned response. It effectively realigned its operational priorities and internal business processes to provide swift, systematic, and concerted support during this period to help India deal with immediate and long-term pandemic impacts.

The Onset of COVID-19 in India

By 2020, India had emerged as one of the two fastest-growing major economies in the world, with average annual gross domestic product growth of 6.3% during 2000–2019 that was accompanied by significant achievements in poverty reduction. The arrival of the pandemic threatened to reverse many of India's hard-won socioeconomic gains. With global economic activity nearly completely stalled by the onset of the pandemic—except for trade in essentials such as food, medicines, and medical supplies—supply chain disruptions caused the partial or total shutdown of manufacturing of most nonessential items for an extended period. Thus, the impacts of the COVID-19 pandemic posed a triple threat to public finances worldwide: (i) a shrinking consumption base, (ii) a reduction in tax income, and (iii) the need for increased government spending on welfare and health care.

The Government of India's response was proactive, preemptive, and graded over different phases of the pandemic. Disease containment, economic relief measures, and vaccine administration were cornerstones of India's COVID-19 management strategy. ADB walked in lockstep with the government to support these measures by effectively realigning its operational priorities and internal business processes.

ADB as India's Long-Standing Development Partner

ADB's effective COVID-19 support to India was facilitated by its long-standing partnership with the Government of India. From 1986 to 2022, ADB committed a total of $60.6 billion to India in the form of public and private sector investments for projects, grants, and technical assistance (TA). ADB support featured most prominently in the following sectors: transport, energy, water and urban infrastructure and services, agriculture and natural resources, health, education and skill development, finance, and public sector management. To maximize its development impact, this support is constantly being realigned with government's evolving priorities and guided by ADB's country partnership strategy (CPS), a regularly updated document that presents a roadmap for ADB operations in India. The latest CPS covering 2023–2027 supports India's national development priorities, among them the attainment of development country status by 2047 when the country marks 100 years of independence. ADB assistance seeks to ensure high, inclusive, and broad-based growth to realize balanced development across all regions, states, and sectors.

Standing with India during the COVID-19 Pandemic

With its large population, India was particularly hard hit by the health and socioeconomic impact of the pandemic. ADB provided much-needed assistance during the critical years of 2020–2021, with its early support focused on strengthening the seven pillars of the government's initial response to COVID-19: (i) testing, (ii) capacity building, (iii) health care infrastructure, (iv) procurement of medical and protective equipment, (v) disease surveillance, (vi) digital tools, and (vii) protocols and guidelines. ADB support also prioritized expanding and strengthening the social security net for low-income and vulnerable populations, including women.

In response to the global crisis, ADB fast-tracked its business processes in March 2020 to swiftly deliver support to developing member countries such as India, setting up a flexible financing instrument called the COVID-19 Pandemic Response Option. As the scale of the crisis became clearer by April 2020, ADB made available up to $20 billion—including $1.5 billion to India—through this instrument to help countries meet emergency needs, provide short-term economic stimulus, and deliver long-term assistance for sustainable recovery.

ADB tailored its COVID-19 program for India to cater to the government's phased approach in dealing with the pandemic. In the initial phase, ADB approved $1.5 billion assistance for the COVID-19 Active Response and Expenditure Support program as budget support to the government's own huge economic relief and emergency response and health system preparedness packages. This aimed to mitigate the adverse health, social, and economic impacts of the pandemic through containment measures and immediate relief to the affected poor, women, and other vulnerable groups. During the subsequent vaccination phase of the pandemic in 2021, ADB approved $1.5 billion in funding to help procure safe and effective vaccines for the benefit of over 300 million Indians.

Since the pandemic had a disproportionate impact in urban areas, ADB focused on increasing access to comprehensive primary health care in urban areas by approving a $300 million program to support the government's flagship initiatives to improve access to health care, especially for the urban poor, in the immediate term and strengthen the health system's capacity for future pandemics over the long term.

To ensure these programs were effectively targeted, ADB provided a TA to strengthen the implementation capacities of relevant ministries and departments. ADB also (i) responded to India's urgent need for crucial medical equipment, providing personal protective equipment and thermal scanners; (ii) improved logistics to streamline the availability of food rations; and (iii) developed e-learning modules for government and health personnel working on the frontlines of pandemic management.

ADB Support to the Private Sector during COVID-19

The spread of the pandemic stretched the capacities of public sector health care facilities across India. To supplement government efforts, ADB provided funding support to scale up the private sector's critical care facilities. Having demonstrated its capability to treat COVID-19 patients at its hospitals' isolation wards and critical care units, Global Health Private Limited (GHPL) was the recipient of a 3-year debt financing package of $20 million from ADB in August 2020. The package enabled GHPL to meet ongoing funding needs and expanded the reach of its much-needed services.

Alongside health and social protection measures to protect citizens was the challenge of sustaining economic activities in the pandemic-ravaged private sector. In several cases, ADB's targeted liquidity support to select private sector companies helped sustain their operations. For example, ADB supported Suguna Foods Private Limited with a loan that allowed the firm to continue its operations and protect the livelihoods of over 40,000 contract poultry farmers. ADB also provided long-term working capital support to ReNew Power Private Limited, a renewable energy producer, to help it maintain operations and meet financing obligations.

Partnering on the Economic Recovery

By the second half of 2021, ADB had shifted gears to focus more on overcoming the economic consequences of COVID-19 and revitalizing India's impressive pre-pandemic growth trends. ADB-approved projects in 2021 and 2022 demonstrated this comprehensive support to India's robust post-pandemic recovery and long-term development priorities. Sustainable health outcomes and urban developmental goals were among the key initiatives that were prioritized.

In addition to its lending and financial aid operations, ADB is helping India forge a path toward developed country status through knowledge support and TA. Strategic studies that rely on evidence-based analyses inform the conceptualization of transformational ADB interventions comprising policy advice, private sector development, and the facilitation of public–private partnerships.

ADB has continued to support the further development of industrial corridors to boost manufacturing, create more jobs, strengthen the skills ecosystem, improve connectivity in rural areas, and upgrade basic urban services. The COVID-19 pandemic most severely impacted informal segments of the economy and deeply affected the health, economic, social, and psychological well-being of women, children, and disadvantaged groups. Women in India faced an outsized burden in terms of increased household responsibilities during the lockdowns, insufficient financial resources for treatment and limited access to health care facilities, and the loss of livelihoods in the women-dominated informal sector. In response, ADB embedded gender equity and social inclusion outcomes into the monitoring framework for all supported activities.

Beyond the Pandemic: The Enduring ADB–India Partnership

The phased support and close engagement of ADB with the Government of India throughout the pandemic reinforced ADB's role as a trusted long-term partner. As part of the ongoing post-pandemic recovery process, India is tackling structural transformation, ameliorating its infrastructure deficit, reducing carbon intensity and climate vulnerability, and addressing socioeconomic inequalities and other long-term development challenges. The COVID-19 pandemic accentuated the need for India to strengthen its health care and social protection systems as well as its education and skills ecosystem for the betterment of all citizens, who are and will remain the country's most valuable resource. Thus, it is natural that ADB's CPS for India, 2023–2027, seeks to facilitate the realization of the government's post-pandemic vision by helping to (i) catalyze robust, private sector-led, green, and inclusive growth; (ii) accelerate structural transformation and job creation; and (iii) promote climate resiliency. As India continues to adapt to post-pandemic economic conditions, ADB will regularly recalibrate its support to help the country fully recover from the impacts of COVID-19 and chart a course toward developed country status.

1   India and the Pandemic

The Pandemic's Onset Disrupts the World

India had emerged as one of the fastest-growing major economies during 2000–2019, reaching average annual gross domestic product (GDP) growth of 6.3%, accompanied by significant poverty reduction,[1] when the coronavirus disease (COVID-19) pandemic (henceforth, the pandemic) swept across the globe at the onset of 2020. India, like with the rest of the world, was caught off-guard by the magnitude of the pandemic that eventually came to reshape socioeconomic priorities and ways of conducting business. The arrival of the pandemic threatened to undo many of India's hard-earned socioeconomic gains.

Records reveal that, in December 2019, the Wuhan Municipal Health Commission in People's Republic of China (PRC) reported a cluster of pneumonia (lung infection) cases of unknown origin in the city of Wuhan. The pneumonia was later identified as the novel coronavirus disease, or COVID-19, which rapidly proliferated to the rest of the world. Countries with significant movements of people across their borders started reporting cases of the disease in January 2020.[2] The World Health Organization (WHO) declared the COVID-19 outbreak a pandemic on 11 March 2020.

During the first half of 2020, the pandemic spread to most countries in the world and brought the global economy to a grinding halt. Governments worldwide put emergency measures in place to deal with the health crisis. The initial pandemic period caught nearly everyone unawares since COVID-19 symptoms are similar to other common illnesses and only a limited supply of testing kits existed in the world. During this period, the number of COVID-19 cases reported globally spiraled exponentially, resulting in a large number of deaths. The initial response focused on containing the spread via isolation through tracking and quarantining, social distancing, and mask-wearing. Many governments put stringent movement restrictions on their citizens and imposed partial or total lockdowns to prevent disease transmission.

Global economic activity stalled except for trade in essentials such as food, medicines, hospital supplies, and other hygiene and health care products and equipment, albeit hampered by logistics and travel restrictions. The disruption of supply chains resulted in the partial or complete halt of manufacturing of most nonessential items. Countries had to resort to emergency funding to meet the basic needs of their poorest citizens. Governments and economies faced a triple threat from (i) a shrinking consumption base, (ii) a reduction in tax income, and (iii) the need for increased government spending on welfare and health care.

---

[1]   World Bank national accounts data and Organisation for Economic Co-operation and Development National Accounts data. https://data.worldbank.org/indicator/NY.GDP.MKTP.KD.ZG?end=2019&locations=IN&start=2000.

[2]   Isaac Ghinai, et al. 2020. First known person-to-person transmission of severe acute respiratory syndrome coronavirus 2 (SARS-CoV-2) in the USA. *The Lancet.* Volume 395. 4 April. https://www.thelancet.com/action/showPdf?pii=S0140-6736%2820%2930607-3.

India, Deeply Impacted

Shops shuttered during pandemic-related lockdown in Sutar chawl, Kalbadevi, Mumbai.

The first case of COVID-19 was detected in India on 30 January 2020 in the southern state of Kerala in a student returning from Wuhan in the PRC. Over the next 2 months, stray cases were reported in Delhi, Jaipur, and Agra. In a bid to control the spread, Prime Minister Narendra Modi announced a 21-day nationwide lockdown on 24 March 2020. It was followed by a series of successive lockdowns spanning 68 days and lasting until 31 May 2020. While the lockdowns substantially controlled the spread of the disease, the complete closure of all commercial and industrial activities and transport impacted daily lives, particularly among poor and vulnerable groups. The urban poor population and migrant workers who depend on daily wages to support their households were left without enough savings or livelihood options. Women were affected by the combined effects of the health crisis, economic fallout, lockdown and associated burdens of home schooling and child and elder care, and an increased incidence of domestic violence.[3] Education was severely disrupted by the closure of schools and colleges for an extended period. With mobility restricted, the lives of those who could afford it (particularly in urban areas), were led through the internet—purchasing household items, conducting online meetings, attending classes, socializing, and consuming entertainment content.

The challenge for governments at this stage was to curb the spread of the disease and swiftly and effectively assist people in distress. Soon after the nationwide lockdown in March 2020, the government announced wide-ranging measures to address the immediate needs of vulnerable groups and strengthen the health care system (section 1.3). With its large population, India would unfortunately be hit particularly hard (Figure 1.1).

---

3   https://www.ohchr.org/sites/default/files/2022-01/india-womens-r-network.pdf.

Figure 1.1   Pandemic Cases and Fatalities (cumulative till 31 August 2023)

Worldwide

Confirmed cases:
770 million

Deaths:
6.96 million

Fatality rate:
0.9%

India

Third-worst-
affected country

Confirmed cases:
45 million

Deaths:
0.53 million

Fatality rate:
1.2%

Source: World Health Organization https://covid19.who.int/region/searo/country/in.

India's Pandemic Response

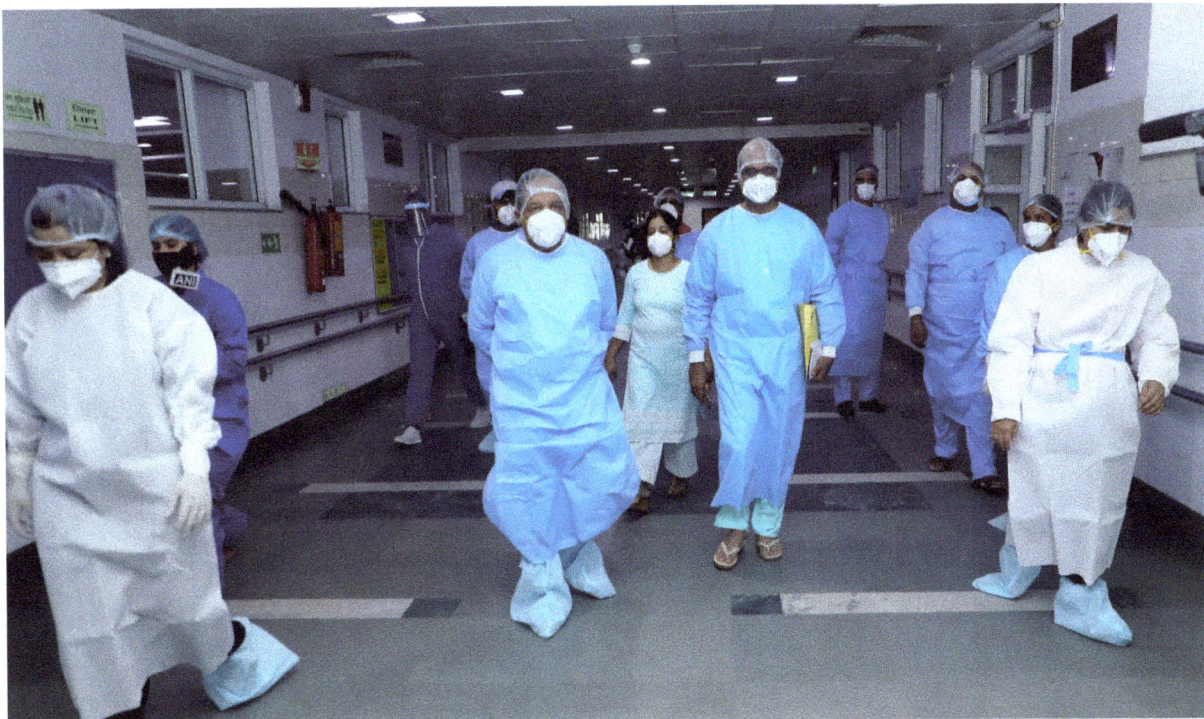

Union Minister of Health and Family Welfare Harsh Vardhan (at the time) along with a medical team overseeing COVID-19 pandemic preparedness in a government-run hospital in Delhi in March 2020.

The Government of India quickly responded to the unfolding challenge. Timely measures included a test, track and treat approach with isolation through containment zones, community surveillance, protocols for home isolation, and effective clinical treatment.

Early containment measures in India included the screening of air travelers from the PRC. Screening was soon extended to travelers from other Southeast Asian countries. In January 2020, India screened over 50,000 travelers and operationalized 12 testing laboratories for COVID-19 samples. In early February 2020, the Government of India constituted a Group of Ministers to coordinate a national response across multiple ministries. In March 2020, as the country saw a gradual rise in cases, India organized training for frontline health officials and other relevant personnel; prohibited flight operations; and announced the closure of educational institutions, gymnasiums, museums, cultural and social centers, swimming pools, and theaters to enforce social distancing norms (Appendix 1).

Between March and May 2020, the government assessed its preparedness and gradually built a comprehensive response mechanism premised on seven pillars (Figure 1.2). It relied on the twin strategy of imposing lockdowns to minimize the spread and simultaneously putting in place measures to test, track, and treat the infected.

It was a time of unprecedented challenge for the government. On the one hand, it needed to immediately respond to the emerging health crisis with an overwhelmed health care system. On the other, it faced the additional responsibility of providing help to poor and most vulnerable citizens who were severely impacted by the pandemic-induced restrictions that disrupted livelihoods and brought economic activity to a virtual standstill.

The government's response was swift. It announced a $2 billion COVID-19 Response and Health Systems Preparedness Package to bolster the health care system during the initial 21-day lockdown,[4] and a longer-term $22.9 billion pro-poor economic relief package under the Pradhan Mantri Garib Kalyan Yojana (PMGKY) on 26 March 2020.[5]

The emergency response and preparedness package had the following mandate:

(i)   procure personal protective equipment, enhance disease surveillance, improve health facilities (including dedicated treatment centers), impart training to health workers, ramp up testing capacity, and enhance tracking for the containment of COVID-19;
(ii)   strengthen national and state health systems to support disease prevention and enhance preparedness;
(iii)   strengthen pandemic research; and
(iv)   enhance risk communication and community engagement.

The economic relief package under PMGKY included measures to expand the social safety net for low-income and vulnerable populations, including women, whose lives and livelihoods were deeply impacted by the pandemic (Table 1.1).

---

[4]   Government of India, Ministry of Health and Family Welfare. 2020. Government of India sanctions Rs. 15000 crores for India COVID-19 Emergency Response and Health System Preparedness Package. Press release through Press Information Bureau. 9 April. https://pib.gov.in/PressReleaseIframePage.aspx?PRID=1612534.

[5]   Government of India, Ministry of Finance. 2020. Finance Minister announces Rs 1.70 Lakh Crore relief package under Pradhan Mantri Garib Kalyan Yojana for the poor to help them fight the battle against Corona Virus. Press release through Press Information Bureau. 26 March. https://pib.gov.in/PressReleaseIframePage.aspx?PRID=1608345.

Figure 1.2   Seven Pillars of the Government of India's Initial Pandemic Response

Testing
- Devised protocols and strategies for testing, accredited testing kits, and approved private labs.
- Identified nodal agency, Indian Council of Medical Research.

Capacity building
- Conducted online courses for frontline workers—doctors, nurses, paramedics, hygiene workers, technicians, state government officers, civil defense officers, police personnel, and other volunteers.

Infrastructure strengthening
- Identified and categorized dedicated COVID-19 hospitals, health centers, and care centers
- Identified 7,740 such facilities in 483 districts by 10 May 2020.[a]
   - As on date, these facilities had 656,769 isolation beds, 305,567 confirmed case beds, 351,204 suspected case beds, 99,492 oxygen supported beds, and 34,076 intensive care beds.

Procurement
- Procured ventilators, oxygen, oxygen cylinders, protective personal equipment, N-95 masks, and diagnostic kits.

Disease surveillance
- Deputized National Center for Disease Control to strengthen disease surveillance and outbreak reporting in India
   - In the initial pandemic phase, the center provided support in contacting travelers and undertaking follow-up on quarantine status through its 24x7 helpline
   - Later, it released guidelines, advisories, and patient information material

Digital tools
- Promoted digital tracking tools such as the Arogya Setu app for self-reporting contact tracing

Guidelines
- Issued periodic advisories and guidelines on COVID-19 management

COVID-19 = coronavirus disease, MOHFW = Ministry of Health and Family Welfare.

[a]   Government of India, Ministry of Health and Family Welfare. 2020. Adequate health infrastructure and health facilities set up for COVID-19 management. Press release through Press Information Bureau. 10 May. https://pib.gov.in/PressReleasePage.aspx?PRID=1622631.

Source: World Health Organization.

Table 1.1 Prominent Components of Pradhan Mantri Garib Kalyan Yojana

	Program	Frequency	Target of Government of India		Cumulative Progress (April 2020–July 2021)	
			Number of beneficiaries (million)	Assistance as of November 2020 (₹ billion)	Number of beneficiaries (million)	Assistance (₹ billion)
1	Insurance cover for health workers	One-time	2.2	0.5	-	14.8
	Insurance cover for ASHAs (all are women)	One-time	2.0	-	1.0	-
2	Pradhan Mantri Garib Kalyan Anna Yojana—Food grains	Once a month for 3 months (extended till November 2020)	800.0 (100% of public distribution system households)	1,489.4	717.8–794.4	1,411.9
	Pradhan Mantri Garib Kalyan Anna Yojana—Pulses		194.0		170.0–183.2	12.0
3	Pradhan Mantri Kisan Samman Nidhi Yojana	Three installments (once every 4 months)	87.0	330.0	-	735.6
4	Mahatma Gandhi National Rural Employment Generation Act (MGNREGA)	100 days of wage employment	136.2 (job card holders)	56.0	5,437.4 (person days)	108.8
5	National Social Assistance Program (for senior citizens, widows, and PWDs)	Two installments	30.0	30.0	-	28.14
6	Pradhan Mantri Jan Dhan Yojana (PMJDY)	Once every month, for 3 months	204.0 (women)	310.0	-	309.5
7	Pradhan Mantri Ujjwala Yojana (for families living below the poverty line)	Once every month, for 3 months (extended till December 2020)	80.2	135.0		97.0
8	Collateral-free loans for self-help groups	-	68.5 (families)	-	5.8 (self-help groups)	976.1
9	Employees' Provident Fund (for organized sector workers)	Once	50.0	-	7.6	187.0
10	Public Provident Fund Scheme—Employees	Once every month, for 3 months (extended till December 2020)	7.8	48.6	3.9	25.7
11	Building and Other Construction Workers Welfare Fund	-	35.0 (registered workers)	310	30.5	74.1
12	Pradhan Mantri Khanij Kshetra Kalyan Yojana (District Mineral Foundation Fund)	30% of the DMF funds COVID-19 relief	-	41.5[a]	-	7.1

ASHA = Accredited Social Health Activist, COVID-19 = coronavirus disease, DMF = District Mineral Foundation, PWD = person with disabilities.

[a] Revised from earlier target of ₹126.2 billion, as Ministry of Mines has clarified that states were allowed to spend up to 30% of the balance funds available with the DMF Fund. As of 21 December 2020, the balance of funds was ₹138.16 billion, 30% of which equals ₹41.5 billion.

Source: Compiled from Appendix 2 of the Project Completion Report (Program Number: 54182-001. Loan Numbers: 3915 and 3916.), *India: COVID-19 Active Response and Expenditure Support Program*, November 2022.

2 ADB as India's Long-Standing Development Partner

India and ADB: Decades of Partnership

The COVID-19 pandemic brought unprecedented health, economic, and social challenges to Asia and the Pacific. Besides the immediate health and socioeconomic adversities, the pandemic also revealed the extent of many entrenched development issues facing the region, including inequalities, socioeconomic insecurities, and environmental challenges.

Since February 2020, ADB's emergency assistance grants to its developing members have helped ensure the supply of essential medicines and personal protective equipment. In April 2020, ADB announced a $20 billion comprehensive response package to help them address the immediate and long-term impacts of the pandemic.

ADB stood by India as the country dealt with the challenges of the pandemic and stepped up to partner with the government in its strategic, multisectoral, and well-planned response. It effectively realigned its operational priorities and internal business processes to provide swift, systematic, and concerted support during this period to help India deal with the immediate and long-term pandemic impacts.

The pace and effectiveness of ADB's pandemic support to India is attributed to the bank's long-standing partnership with the country. India is among ADB's founding members and is now its fourth-largest shareholder. ADB has been a close partner in India's development efforts during the different phases of its economic growth, aligning ADB's initiatives with the country's evolving needs and priorities.

ADB's first set of operations in India helped facilitate the economic reform agenda of the early 1990s, including aid to infrastructure development and support for the foreign exchange requirements of opening to international trade. Over the years, ADB's India program has developed and matured in terms of its sectoral, geographic, and thematic coverage to reflect the country's evolving development priorities.

From the commencement of its lending operations to India in 1986 through 2022, ADB committed a total of $60.6 billion in public and private sector investments for projects, grants, and technical assistance (TA). The most prominent sectors in terms of ADB support to India are transport, energy, urban infrastructure and services (including water), finance, agriculture, natural resources and rural development, health, education, and public sector management (Table 2.1).[6]

---

[6] Asian Development Bank. Member Factsheet. April 2023. https://www.adb.org/sites/default/files/publication/27768/ind-2022.pdf.

Table 2.1   The Asian Development Bank's Cumulative India Commitments, 1986–2022

Sector	No.	Amount ($ billion)	% of Total
Project and Technical Assistance	**855**	**59.70**	**98.5**
Agriculture, natural resources, and rural development	63	2.15	3.55
Education	20	0.65	1.07
Energy	214	14.96	24.68
Finance	92	6.19	10.21
Health	20	2.16	3.56
Industry and trade	21	0.77	1.27
Information and communication technology	3	0.15	0.25
Multisector	30	2.14	3.53
Public sector management	76	3.61	5.96
Transport	197	20.24	33.4
Water and other urban infrastructure and services	119	6.67	11.01
Trade and Supply Chain Finance Program and Microfinance Program	**1,378**	**0.91**	**1.5**
Finance	1,200	0.89	1.47
Industry and trade	178	0.02	0.03
Total	**2,233**	**60.60**	**100**

DMC = developing member country, TA = technical assistance.

Notes:

1. Commitments include loans, grants, equity investments, guarantees, technical assistance (TA), and private sector programs.
2. Grants and TA include ADB-administered cofinancing.
3. Using primary sector in the reporting of commitments.
4. From 2020, financing for TA projects with regional coverage is distributed to their specific DMCs where breakdowns are available.
5. Commitments under Trade and Supply Chain Finance Program and Microfinance Program include ADB-financed commitments from private sector programs, of which $615.6 million comprises short-term financing (maturity of less than 365 days).
6. Amount may not sum precisely because of rounding.

Source: Asian Development Bank. Member Factsheet, April 2023. https://www.adb.org/sites/default/files/publication/27768/ind-2022.pdf.

To maximize development impact, ADB aligns its assistance with the priorities of the Government of India, lending support to the government's development goals, policy programs, and welfare measures. This support is guided by the country partnership strategy (CPS), a regularly updated document that presents a roadmap for ADB operations in India. The CPS for 2023–2027 supports India's national development priorities, among which the "attainment of developed country status by 2047, the 100th year of Indian independence" figures prominently. This can be achieved through technology-driven development that promotes energy transition and climate action, and the creation of a virtuous cycle of public capital investment crowding in private investments to foster innovation.

Strengthening the ADB–India Partnership in the Midst of the Pandemic

The spread of the pandemic overwhelmed India's health care system while the pandemic-induced restrictions disrupted economic activity and livelihoods. The Government of India adopted a multipronged COVID-19 management strategy to address these challenges. It responded proactively to augment preventive and therapeutic health care centers, diagnostic and research facilities, and tracking services, which was followed by a nationwide vaccination campaign to minimize the loss of human life. Simultaneously, the government announced successive stimulus packages to provide immediate relief to the citizens, especially poor and vulnerable sections, and to help businesses and industries to sustain their operations to help India's economic recovery.

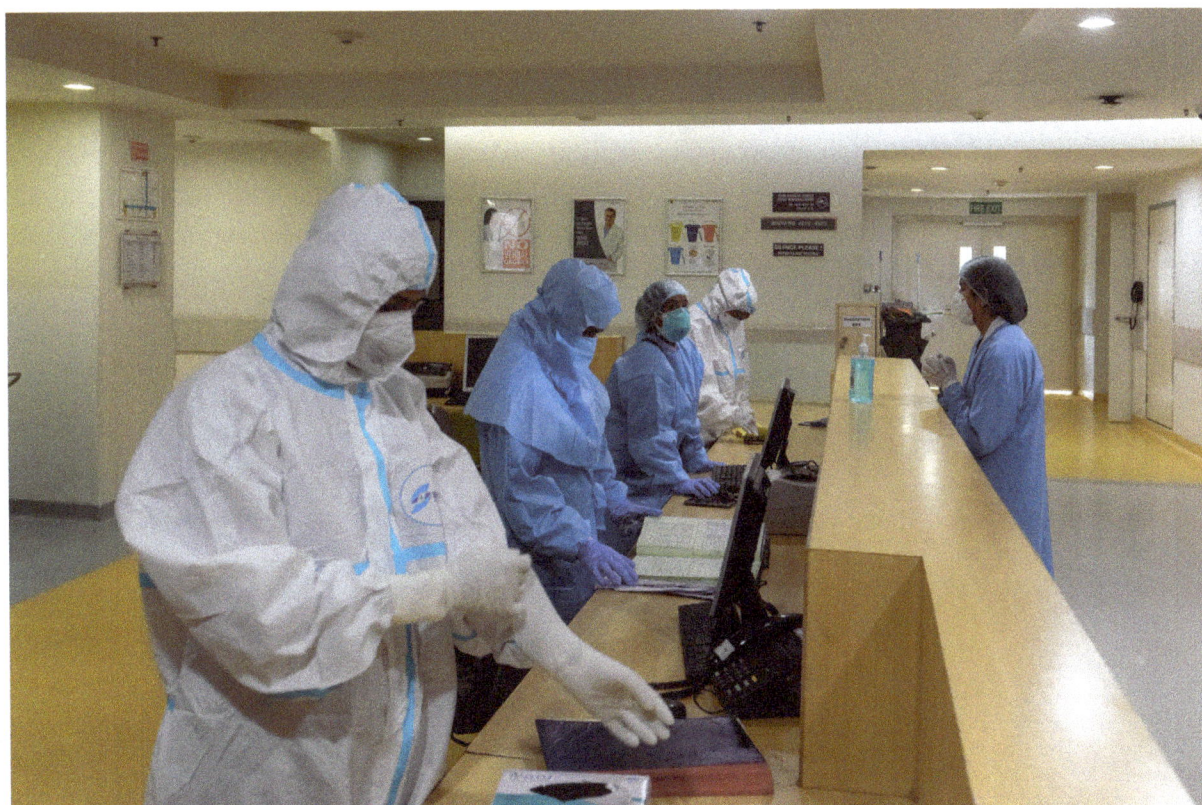

ADB supported procurement of medical equipment and personal protective equipment for use at medical facilities.

As a long-term partner in India's development journey, ADB worked closely with the government to support its pandemic response. The situation demanded a shift away from ADB's business-as-usual approach so that it could fast-track assistance to buttress India's fight against the pandemic. Accordingly, ADB streamlined its internal business processes to assist the government's COVID-19 management strategy across different phases while continuing its regular operations in the country.

By April 2020, ADB had fast-tracked and made available $1.5 billion as budget support for the government's pro-poor economic relief package and the health system preparedness package. ADB approved an additional $1.5 billion in 2021 to finance the procurement of safe and effective vaccines.

Due to the pandemic's significant impact in urban areas, ADB worked to increase access to comprehensive primary health care among the urban poor people and improve the health system's resiliency in the face of future pandemics. Other support included TA to strengthen the targeting and implementation capacities of key ministries and departments through improved logistics and the development of e-learning modules for those working on the pandemic's frontlines. ADB also supported procurement of medical equipment and personal protective equipment for use at medical facilities and thermal scanners at ports of entry.

India's public health care facilities were severely taxed by the spread of COVID-19, which led ADB to scale up the private sector's critical care facilities to supplement public sector capacities. This included the August 2020 awarding of a 3-year debt financing package worth $20 million to a private sector health care provider. The funds enabled the firm to both meet the huge increase in funding requirements caused by the pandemic and expand the capacities and reach of its various health services. In other instances, ADB provided direct liquidity support to sustain the operations of private sector companies such as a poultry supplier and a renewable energy producer. ADB also renewed its support for the Government of India's industrial corridor development program, which aims to establish multimodal logistics parks and economic corridors as manufacturing-led growth engines linking key domestic economic centers with regional and global supply chains.

Projects approved in 2021 and 2022 by ADB signaled its continued support to India's sustainable recovery in the post-pandemic era. ADB is also extending knowledge support and technical assistance—including evidence-based studies and policy advice—and facilitating public–private partnerships to maximize investments in India's long-term development. Since the COVID-19 pandemic most severely impacted informal segments of the economy—particularly women, children, and disadvantaged groups among them—gender equity and social inclusion outcomes were incorporated into the monitoring frameworks of all ADB-supported activities.

The design, outputs, outcomes, and impacts of the aforementioned ADB projects, as well as several others that provided support to the Government of India's COVID-19 pandemic response, will be discussed in more detail in subsequent sections of this report.

3 Standing with India during the Pandemic

A Flexible Approach to a Rapidly Evolving Crisis

As with other multilateral development banks, 2020–2021 was an unprecedented period for ADB. The COVID-19 pandemic not only challenged the operations of ongoing projects but also precipitated a shift in assistance priorities, with emphasis being placed on strengthening health care and public distribution systems (PDS), enhancing vaccine coverage, and creating livelihood opportunities.

Given the enormity of the challenge posed by COVID-19, ADB moved swiftly to deliver support to its developing member countries (DMCs), rapidly setting up a flexible financing instrument called the COVID-19 Pandemic Response Option (CPRO) to help governments protect poor and vulnerable groups. As the scale of the crisis became clearer, in April 2020, ADB expanded its initial allocation for the COVID-19 response and made available up to $20 billion to help its DMCs meet emergency needs, provide short-term economic stimulus, and deliver longer-term assistance for sustainable recovery. ADB also provided support for the private sector in the form of increased assistance to strengthen trade and supply chains.

ADB fast-tracked improvements to its business processes, including encouraging online systems for procurement and bidding to ensure swift project approval and implementation.

Shifting Gears to Address the Pandemic Impact in India

ADB's phased approach to support the Government of India's pandemic response started at the initial phase of the pandemic spread. ADB swiftly approved the COVID-19 Active Response and Expenditure Support (CARES) program under its CPRO modality to provide budget support to the government's economic package aimed at immediate health and social protection measures. In addition to strengthening the health system, the program targeted last-mile beneficiaries such as health workers, informal workers (particularly migrants in urban and peri-urban areas), and women and other disadvantaged groups who required immediate support to the economic shocks. In tandem with the government's priority of strengthening comprehensive health care in urban areas that were hardest hit by the initial phase of the pandemic, ADB approved an assistance program to expand health care services in urban primary health centers and health and wellness centers across multiple states for both COVID-19 and non-COVID-19 care. These interventions were complemented by the ADB grant assistance to finance (i) the procurement of thermal scanners and personal protective equipment, (ii) TA for effective implementation of health sector and social protection measures supported through the CARES program, and (iii) assistance to the "COVID-19 War Room" set up in the Ministry of Health and Family Welfare (MOHFW) for monitoring the pandemic's spread across the country. ADB also helped the government operationalize an

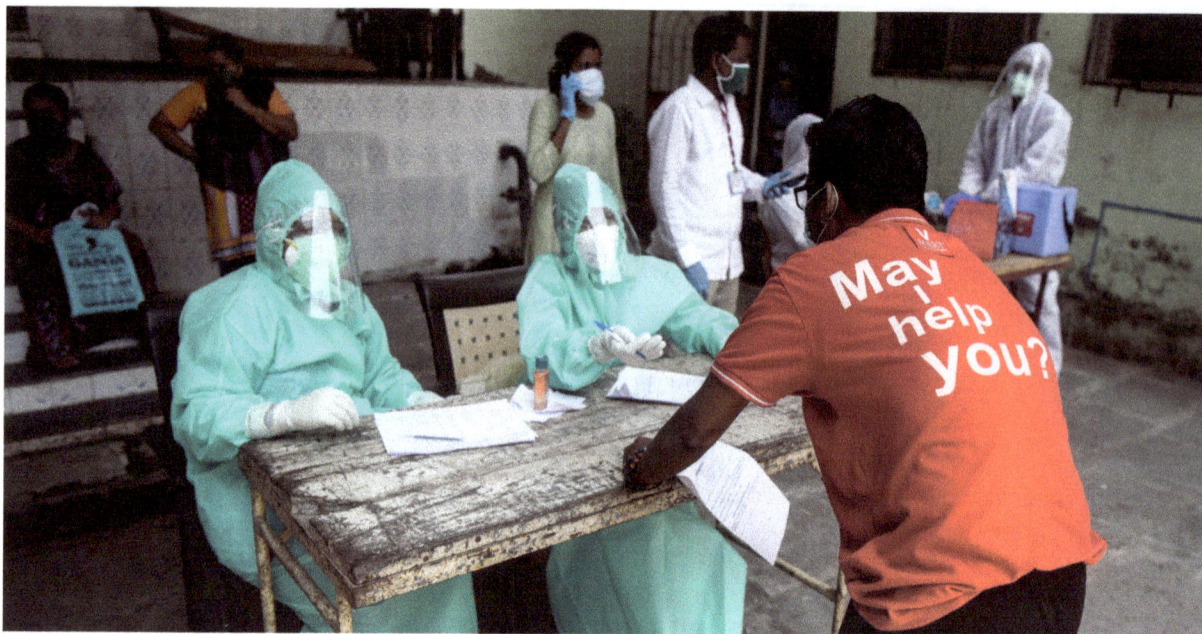

Medical officers interact with a volunteer during a coronavirus testing drive.

Integrated Government Online Training scheme through e-learning modules to train civil servants who were carrying out pandemic relief operations as frontline workers.[7]

In the next phase of the pandemic, as India launched a large-scale countrywide vaccination program targeted to reduce the severity of COVID-19 hospitalizations and deaths, ADB approved funding to enable India to procure safe and effective vaccines for the benefit of over 300 million people. This effort was aligned to ADB's $9 billion Asia Pacific Vaccine Access Facility (APVAX) launched in December 2020 to assist DMCs in the rapid procurement and delivery of effective and safe COVID-19 vaccines in an equitable manner. ADB also provided funding support to Global Health Private Limited that helped scale up the private sector's critical COVID-19 care facilities, thereby further strengthening India's battle against the pandemic.

By the second half of 2021, ADB had again shifted gears to help India overcome the economic consequences of the COVID-19 pandemic, supporting projects to aid the post-pandemic recovery process. Some of these ADB investments were targeted to

- facilitate industrial corridor development and industrial policy reforms to re-catalyze supply chains disrupted during to the pandemic,
- support skills development to promote employability amid the changed nature of work after the pandemic,
- promote urban reforms to expand access to basic health and hygiene facilities, and
- enhance rural connectivity and agriculture investments to mitigate rural distress.

While ADB's assistance supported the Government of India's evolving priorities over different phases of COVID-19, it was also targeted to support several private sector interventions to meet immediate working capital needs of companies to sustain their operations that were impacted by the pandemic spread (Table 3.1).

Detailed discussions follow on programs related to ADB support for India's COVID-19 response, covering objectives, outputs, outcomes, and impacts.

---

[7]   For details please see Box 6.2.

Table 3.1   ADB's Phased Support to India's COVID-19 Pandemic Response

ADB Support	Value ($ million)	Purpose
Immediate Pandemic Support		
1 COVID-19 Active Response and Expenditure Support (CARES) program, April 2020	1,500	Feed into the government's $2.0 billion COVID-19 Response and Health Systems Preparedness package and $22.9 billion pro-poor economic relief package—Pradhan Mantri Garib Kalyan Yojana (PMGKY)
Technical Assistance (TA), April 2020	2	TA attached to CARES for targeting beneficiaries with focus on poor households and women
Grant under Asia Pacific Disaster Response Fund, July 2020	3	Grant to the United Nations Children's Fund to procure thermal scanners for COVID-19 detection at ports and airports
2 Strengthening Comprehensive Primary Health Care in Urban Areas Program, November 2020	300	Support the Pradhan Mantri Ayushman Bharat Health Infrastructure Mission to strengthen comprehensive primary health care in urban areas
3 Debt Financing Global Health Private Limited, August 2020	20	Finance Global Health Private Limited to strengthen private sector health care response to the contagion
4 Debt Financing Suguna Foods Private Limited, June 2020	10	Finance Suguna Foods Private Limited as a private sector intervention to support MSMEs providing livelihood activities for rural poor populations and women—Sustaining Poultry Farmer Income and Food Security Project in India
5 Debt Financing ReNew Power Private Limited, July 2020	50	Support to ReNew Power Private Limited to helps sustain its operations as provider of an essential service
Assistance for Controlling the Contagion		
6 Responsive COVID-19 Vaccines for Recovery Project, November 2021	1,500	Financial support for vaccine procurement and distribution
Partnering in the Recovery		
7 Policy-based loan (PBL) for Industrial Corridor Development Program (Subprogram 1), October 2021	250	Strengthen the corridors' institutional structures and formulate mechanisms for integrated development; first of two subprograms for the development of five existing and six new industrial corridors
8 Assam Skill University Project (loan and TA), November 2021	112	Strengthen the industry-aligned flexible skills education and training system in Assam to meet the changing nature of work highlighted by the pandemic
9 PBL for Sustainable Urban Development and Service Delivery Program, November 2021 (Subprogram 1)	350	Improve urban service delivery, accelerate nationwide urban reforms, enhance funding to the urban sector, address low financial capacity of urban local bodies, and improve governance frameworks to speed up private sector participation in urban services delivery
10 Additional financing for Maharashtra Rural Connectivity Improvement Project, July 2021	300	Scale up improvements to rural connectivity through an additional 1,100 (climate-resilient, all-weather) roads and 230 bridges, totaling 2,900 kilometer in 34 districts of Maharashtra state

ADB = Asian Development Bank; COVID-19 = coronavirus disease; MSMEs = micro, small, and medium-sized enterprises.

Source: Asian Development Bank.

Immediate Pandemic Support—CARES Plus

Overview of the CARES Plus Program

ADB approved $1.5 billion of assistance under the CARES program as budget support to the government's $22.9 billion economic relief package through PMGKY and the $2 billion COVID-19 Emergency Response and Health Systems Preparedness Package in April 2020. The CARES program consisted of two back-to-back loans of $500 million and $1 billion that provided urgent budget support for creating the requisite fiscal space to act quickly and finance additional critical expenditures to control the COVID-19 spread. To ensure effective delivery and implementation, the program was supplemented by a $2 million TA to achieve two key outcomes: (i) increased uptake of portability transactions using the One Nation One Ration Card (ONORC) and (ii) evaluation of the Pradhan Mantri Ujjwala Yojana (PMUY), a scheme providing free cooking gas cylinders to women from below poverty line (BPL) households.

During the CPRO loan preparation process, ADB remained involved in policy dialogues on the economic impact of the response to the pandemic by joining meetings chaired by the Department of Economic Affairs (DEA) of the Government of India and recommended measures that added value to the government's response plan. In addition to working closely with the DEA and several central government ministries, including the Ministry of Health and Family Welfare, tasked with pandemic control measures, ADB also coordinated with international partners for its pandemic response programs. These included the International Monetary Fund for immediate support based on its assessment of COVID-19's impact on the Indian economy; the United Nations Children's Fund (UNICEF) for supplying emergency equipment; and the World Health Organization (WHO) on the technical aspects of India's pandemic response. The assistance was synchronized with and complemented the World Bank's $1.0 billion PMGKY assistance and similar initiatives by other country programs.[8]

ADB support was further supplement by a $3 million grant to immediately procure mass thermal scanners at international airports and seaports for the quick detection of fever. Taken together, these various interventions, which are referred to collectively as "CARES Plus" in this report, comprised the fulcrum of ADB's immediate support to India's COVID-19 pandemic response (Figure 3.1).

Objective of the CARES Plus Program

The program's overarching objective was to provide budgetary support to the government's emergency health and social protection measures to help contain COVID-19 transmission and minimize adverse economic, public, and social impacts.

Key Outputs of CARES Plus Support in India

The CARES program had three key outputs:[9]

(i)   implementation of COVID-19 response and health system measures,
(ii)   enhancement of social assistance to compensate for economic losses among vulnerable groups, and
(iii) strengthening of social security measures for affected workers in both the organized and informal sectors.

Most indicators under the CARES program pertaining to health system measures and the government's PMGKY pro-poor relief package exceeded targets. Other targets were "achieved" or "substantially achieved" (Figure 3.2).

---

[8]   Other assistance programs offering support to India's COVID-19 response included Agence Française de Développement, Asian Infrastructure Investment Bank, Japan International Cooperation Agency, Kreditanstalt für Wiederaufbau, and the Center for Disease Control and Prevention in United States.

[9]   Compiled from the Project Completion Report (Program Number: 54182-001. Loan Numbers: 3915 and 3916.), *India: COVID-19 Active Response and Expenditure Support Program*, November 2022.

Figure 3.1   CARES Plus—Motivating Factors in India

CARES = COVID-19 Active Response and Expenditure Support, COVID-19 = coronavirus disease, GOI = Government of India.
Source: Asian Development Bank.

ADB Technical Assistance to Strengthen CARES Plus Implementation

ADB provided a grant-based transaction TA (CARES TA) to strengthen the government's operational framework and promote efficient implementation, monitoring, and evaluation of its health sector programs and pro-poor economic packages in the pandemic context (Box 3.1). In the health sector, the TA supported MOHFW in comprehensive assessment, planning, implementation, and monitoring of COVID-19 response across India; policy formulation for medical oxygen sufficiency; raising awareness among communities to drive engagement; and promoting health innovations, including telemedicine for home-based care. To enhance the impact of social protection measures, the TA helped build the capacity of select implementing agencies in improving the efficiency of PMGKY schemes such as the distribution of free rations and delivery of free cooking gas cylinders through effective targeting, delivery, and monitoring and evaluation. One of the key activities under the CARES TA was a survey on the uptake, implementation, portability, and operability of the ONORC scheme, which was preceded by a diagnostic study on PDS implementation in Madhya Pradesh.

Figure 3.2   Key Outputs under ADB's Support to India via CARES

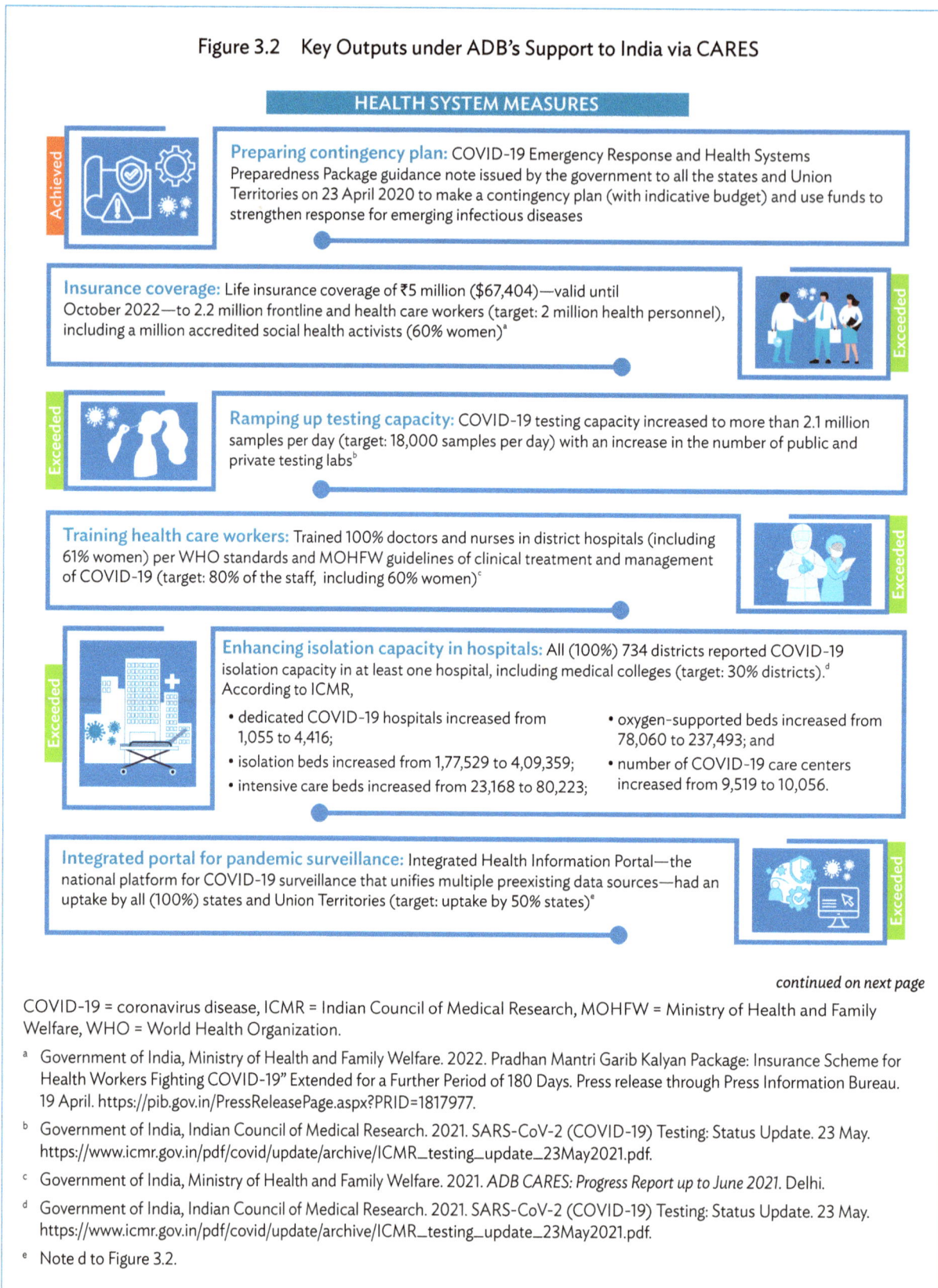

HEALTH SYSTEM MEASURES

Achieved

Preparing contingency plan: COVID-19 Emergency Response and Health Systems Preparedness Package guidance note issued by the government to all the states and Union Territories on 23 April 2020 to make a contingency plan (with indicative budget) and use funds to strengthen response for emerging infectious diseases

Insurance coverage: Life insurance coverage of ₹5 million ($67,404)—valid until October 2022—to 2.2 million frontline and health care workers (target: 2 million health personnel), including a million accredited social health activists (60% women)[a]

Exceeded

Exceeded

Ramping up testing capacity: COVID-19 testing capacity increased to more than 2.1 million samples per day (target: 18,000 samples per day) with an increase in the number of public and private testing labs[b]

Training health care workers: Trained 100% doctors and nurses in district hospitals (including 61% women) per WHO standards and MOHFW guidelines of clinical treatment and management of COVID-19 (target: 80% of the staff, including 60% women)[c]

Exceeded

Exceeded

Enhancing isolation capacity in hospitals: All (100%) 734 districts reported COVID-19 isolation capacity in at least one hospital, including medical colleges (target: 30% districts).[d] According to ICMR,

- dedicated COVID-19 hospitals increased from 1,055 to 4,416;
- isolation beds increased from 1,77,529 to 4,09,359;
- intensive care beds increased from 23,168 to 80,223;
- oxygen-supported beds increased from 78,060 to 237,493; and
- number of COVID-19 care centers increased from 9,519 to 10,056.

Integrated portal for pandemic surveillance: Integrated Health Information Portal—the national platform for COVID-19 surveillance that unifies multiple preexisting data sources—had an uptake by all (100%) states and Union Territories (target: uptake by 50% states)[e]

Exceeded

continued on next page

COVID-19 = coronavirus disease, ICMR = Indian Council of Medical Research, MOHFW = Ministry of Health and Family Welfare, WHO = World Health Organization.

a   Government of India, Ministry of Health and Family Welfare. 2022. Pradhan Mantri Garib Kalyan Package: Insurance Scheme for Health Workers Fighting COVID-19" Extended for a Further Period of 180 Days. Press release through Press Information Bureau. 19 April. https://pib.gov.in/PressReleasePage.aspx?PRID=1817977.

b   Government of India, Indian Council of Medical Research. 2021. SARS-CoV-2 (COVID-19) Testing: Status Update. 23 May. https://www.icmr.gov.in/pdf/covid/update/archive/ICMR_testing_update_23May2021.pdf.

c   Government of India, Ministry of Health and Family Welfare. 2021. *ADB CARES: Progress Report up to June 2021*. Delhi.

d   Government of India, Indian Council of Medical Research. 2021. SARS-CoV-2 (COVID-19) Testing: Status Update. 23 May. https://www.icmr.gov.in/pdf/covid/update/archive/ICMR_testing_update_23May2021.pdf.

e   Note d to Figure 3.2.

Figure 3.2 *continued*

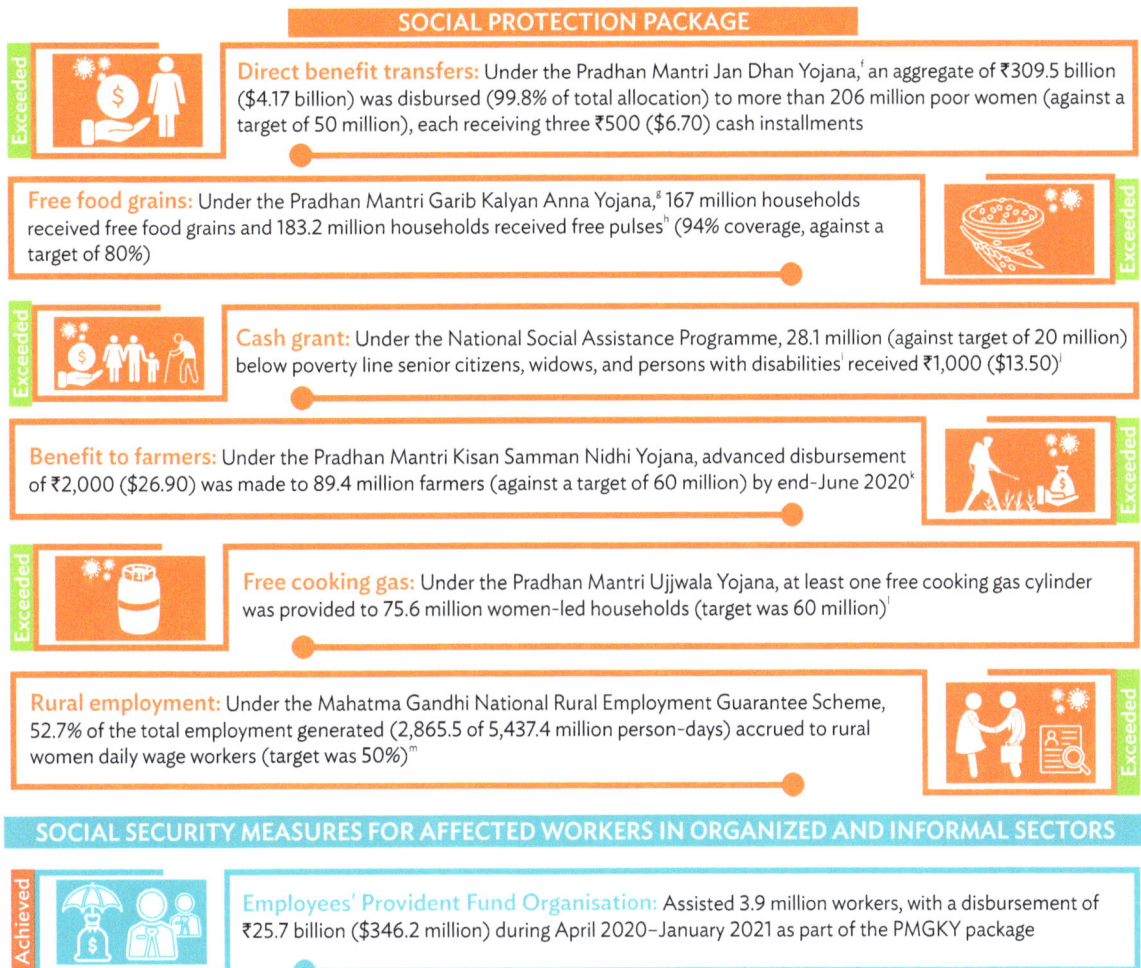

SOCIAL PROTECTION PACKAGE

Exceeded — **Direct benefit transfers:** Under the Pradhan Mantri Jan Dhan Yojana,[f] an aggregate of ₹309.5 billion ($4.17 billion) was disbursed (99.8% of total allocation) to more than 206 million poor women (against a target of 50 million), each receiving three ₹500 ($6.70) cash installments

Free food grains: Under the Pradhan Mantri Garib Kalyan Anna Yojana,[g] 167 million households received free food grains and 183.2 million households received free pulses[h] (94% coverage, against a target of 80%) — *Exceeded*

Exceeded — **Cash grant:** Under the National Social Assistance Programme, 28.1 million (against target of 20 million) below poverty line senior citizens, widows, and persons with disabilities[i] received ₹1,000 ($13.50)[j]

Benefit to farmers: Under the Pradhan Mantri Kisan Samman Nidhi Yojana, advanced disbursement of ₹2,000 ($26.90) was made to 89.4 million farmers (against a target of 60 million) by end-June 2020[k] — *Exceeded*

Exceeded — **Free cooking gas:** Under the Pradhan Mantri Ujjwala Yojana, at least one free cooking gas cylinder was provided to 75.6 million women-led households (target was 60 million)[l]

Rural employment: Under the Mahatma Gandhi National Rural Employment Guarantee Scheme, 52.7% of the total employment generated (2,865.5 of 5,437.4 million person-days) accrued to rural women daily wage workers (target was 50%)[m] — *Exceeded*

SOCIAL SECURITY MEASURES FOR AFFECTED WORKERS IN ORGANIZED AND INFORMAL SECTORS

Achieved — **Employees' Provident Fund Organisation:** Assisted 3.9 million workers, with a disbursement of ₹25.7 billion ($346.2 million) during April 2020–January 2021 as part of the PMGKY package

[f] Government of India, Ministry of Finance. 2021. 41.94 crore accounts opened under Pradhan Mantri Jan Dhan Yojana. Press release through Press Information Bureau. 15 March. https://pib.gov.in/PressReleaseIframePage.aspx?PRID=1704874.

[g] Ministry of Consumer Affairs, Food and Public Distribution, Government of India.

[h] The average household size is 4.8 persons, per the 2011 census. Government of India.

[i] Letter No. L-11014/01/2017 – NSAP, Government of India, Ministry of Rural Development, (National Social Assistance Programme Division) dated 23 November 2020. Disaggregated data: (i) 21.4 million senior citizens received ₹214.3 billion ($2.9 billion) in benefits; (ii) 5.9 million widows received ₹5.9 billion ($80.1 million) in financial benefits; and (iii) 0.8 million differently-abled persons received ₹773 million ($10.4 million) in financial benefits.

[j] Note i to Figure 3.2.

[k] Ministry of Agriculture and Farmers Welfare, Government of India.

[l] Data as on 8 March 2021. Ministry of Petroleum and Natural Gas, Government of India.

[m] Government of India, Ministry of Rural Development. The Mahatma Gandhi National Rural Employment Guarantee Act. https://mnregaweb4.nic.in/netnrega/demand_emp_demand.aspx?lflag=eng&file1=empprov&fin=2020-2021&fin_year=2020-2021&source=national&Digest=KAH+atXWjMgUk3rFXMFZsQ. | Government of India, Ministry of Rural Development. 2021. The Government allocated ₹73,000 crore for MGNREGS for FY 2021–22; an increase of ₹11,500 crore as compared to the FY2021. Press release through Press Information Bureau. 27 July. https://pib.gov.in/PressReleasePage.aspx?PRID=1739616.

Source: Asian Development Bank.

Box 3.1   CARES Program Helps Provide Succor to Millions

For the common citizen, the initial phase of the pandemic brought numerous hardships. The Government of India announced immediate relief measures in March 2020 to help poor people and strengthen national and state health systems' capacity to respond to the pandemic.

"I had to face many challenges during the COVID-19 pandemic. We could not go out due to the lockdown and our household budget was completely upset," says Sarita Kanojiya, a wage worker who was among many that lost their livelihoods. "The government gave us free rations and cooking gas cylinders, and we felt relieved and were able to survive."

Munni Devi, a housewife in Uttar Pradesh's Miyaganj village, recalls the hardships posed by the pandemic: "The pandemic caused a lot of problems for us. There was a lockdown and curfew. We could not get anything to eat or drink… we could not go out. Then the government took note and supplied us will all kinds of provisions—rations, cooking oil, rice, flour… everything."

Millions of such households benefited from the Prime Minister Garib Kalyan Yojana (PMGKY), which helped them overcome the adverse socioeconomic impacts of the pandemic. ADB's CARES Plus program supported the government's relief package under PMGKY and strengthened the preparedness of the health system.

Millions like Sarita Kanojiya (left), a wage worker in Uttar Pradesh's NOIDA district, and Munni Devi (right), a housewife in Uttar Pradesh's Miyaganj village, were able to weather pandemic-induced restrictions with government's immediate relief package.
Source: Asian Development Bank.

A.   Support to Health Sector Initiatives under CARES TA

To support the implementation of the government's health sector preparedness measures, the CARES TA assisted in strengthening national pandemic monitoring procedures and guidelines, bolstering COVID-19 care infrastructure, and enhancing community awareness and preparedness.

Support for comprehensive pandemic monitoring and community outreach. ADB provided support for assessment, planning, implementation, and monitoring of the government's nationwide COVID-19 response across four critical tracks detailed below:

- Track 1 involved monitoring of COVID-19 across India's 734 districts, timely identification of emerging hotspots, monitoring responses instituted by various state governments, and support in drafting guidelines and standard operating procedures. ADB provided support to MOHFW for operationalizing its central "COVID-19 War Room" that was established to track the pandemic's spread with daily and weekly assessments.
- Track 2 included developing several data analytic dashboards to augment COVID-19 monitoring system with real time and data-driven decision making.

Daily tracking of the pandemic spread by the National COVID-19 Monitoring Center, Ministry of Health and Family Welfare, New Delhi.

- Track 3 led to the integration of data analytic with Co-WIN application (a platform to manage and update vaccine status).
- Track 4 was related to the establishment and operation of an Integrated Control and Command Center for current and future emergency medical response needs.

Separately, ADB also provided technical support to an Oxygen-Program Management Unit located in the MOHFW, including policy formulation advice to ensure appropriate medical oxygen sufficiency across the country. To promote home-based care support for COVID-19 patients, ADB supported a Telemedicine Cell that catered to the needs of asymptomatic and mild COVID-19 infected patients with a view to manage sudden surge of pandemic cases.

Enhancing community awareness. Reaching out to communities was important to dispel prevailing myths about COVID-19, enhance awareness of relevant services, and ensure preventive actions and vaccination. ADB coordinated with national institutes such as the Public Health Foundation of India and Tata Institute of Social Sciences and local nongovernment organizations (NGOs) such as Sambodhi to support community outreach in major urban centers such as Mumbai, Bengaluru, and Delhi, particularly in informal settlements. In Mumbai, ADB facilitated the establishment of community-based care centers, assessed community needs through a survey of over 35,000 households, and mapped available services to facilitate increased community access. In Bengaluru, ADB

A pandemic care outreach session in Mumbai.

supported a study in informal settlements that revealed the socioeconomic fallout of the pandemic had resulted in disturbances to mental health, depression, and even suicides.[10] Authorities were apprised of these findings to integrate mental health and wellness, especially among women, into the government's pandemic response.

B.   Support to Social Protection Measures under CARES TA

The CARES TA supported the government in implementing its social protection measures under PMGKY by undertaking various studies. This included a study on enhancing uptake of foodgrains and other commodities available under PDS through the nationally portable ration card. ADB also supported Essential Commodity Price Monitoring and Analysis aimed at identifying gaps across 114 Price Monitoring Division centers and build staff capacity for efficient price monitoring and digital tracking to strengthen implementation of schemes such as PMGKY.

Increasing the uptake of transactions using a nationally portable ration card. Nearly 800 million people in India were eligible to receive free food grains and pulses during the COVID-19 pandemic under the government's food security welfare scheme. These rations were allocated to individual ration cards and delivered through the elaborate PDS via local fair price shops (FPSs) during April–November 2020. However, claiming free or subsidized rations for migrant workers living away from their permanent homes posed a challenge. Owing to the defined coverage of beneficiaries in each state under the National Food Security Act, 2013, it was difficult for migrant beneficiaries to get a new ration card issued in a different state. The government introduced portability of ration cards to meet this need gap (Box 3.2).

To help the government expand the reach of the ONORC scheme and its uptake among beneficiaries, ADB conducted a study to identify key issues and challenges in its implementation and recommend ways to address them.

---

[10]   B. Sahu, T. Sathyanarayana, Giridhara R. Babu, S. Shapeti, S. Queeny, H.B. Dubasi, Deepa R., N.D. Saldanha, R. Bhatia, and S. Khetrapal. 2022. Suicide during pandemic requires deeper engagement. *Asian Journal of Psychiatry*. July, 73, 103161.

Box 3.2   One Nation One Ration Card

To address the difficulties of providing rations to migrant workers, the government introduced the intrastate and interstate portability of ration cards through a technology-driven system called One Nation One Ration Card (ONORC). A similar scheme had been launched as a pilot in 2019 in four states—Gujarat, Maharashtra, Andhra Pradesh, and Telangana. The pandemic prompted the fast-tracking of the nationwide rollout of ONORC, which meant that all eligible ration card holders could now access their entitlement of food grains from any FPS across the country enabled with an e-POS device.

e-POS instrument

Beneficiaries collecting food grains during the pandemic from an FPS at Burdwan, West Bengal

Migrant workers being briefed on the ONORC in Delhi.

continued on next page

Box 3.2   *continued*

Furthermore, while the migrant beneficiary could collect rations at the destination state through the portability function, their family back home could also collect their portion of the entitled ration from the home FPS. The scheme proved beneficial to a large number of migrant workers, with around 22 million portability transactions recorded every month between March 2021 and August 2021 (Figure B3.1).

Figure B3.1   Benefits of the One Nation One Ration Card Scheme

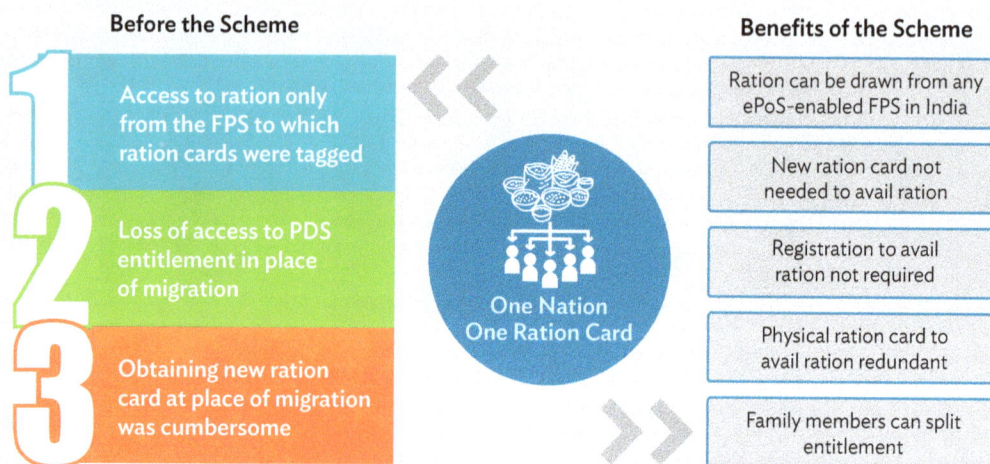

Before the Scheme

1. Access to ration only from the FPS to which ration cards were tagged
2. Loss of access to PDS entitlement in place of migration
3. Obtaining new ration card at place of migration was cumbersome

One Nation One Ration Card

Benefits of the Scheme

- Ration can be drawn from any ePoS-enabled FPS in India
- New ration card not needed to avail ration
- Registration to avail ration not required
- Physical ration card to avail ration redundant
- Family members can split entitlement

ePoS = electronic point-of-sale, FPS = fair price shop, PDS = public distribution system.
Source: Asian Development Bank.

On 6 October 2022, Sudhanshu Pandey, Secretary, Department of Food and Public Distribution, Government of India, marked the launch of an ADB-supported study on the uptake of portable rations under the ONORC scheme.

To assess the progress of the scheme's implementation from the perspective of all stakeholders, the ADB study was conducted among migrants, nonmigrants, FPS dealers, and government stakeholders at the national and state levels.[11]

The study ultimately recommended (i) increasing awareness to expand the base and utilization of the ONORC facility by migrant workers through special drives and targeted campaigns; (ii) building the capacity of the dealers and PDS officials on various aspects of ONORC; (iii) upgrading technological infrastructure, upgrading electronic point-of-sale devices, and increasing server capacity for FPS to better cope with the transaction load; (iv) strengthening the rations supply chain by advancing the lifting of food grains, allocating buffer stocks at FPSs, and streaming delays in ration distribution; and (v) improving access for women and vulnerable groups through increased digital literacy and targeted awareness campaigns.

Free cooking gas cylinders to women from households living below the poverty line. The provision of free cooking gas cylinders to BPL families under the Pradhan Mantri Ujjwala Yojana (PMUY) scheme was an important part of the government's COVID-19 economic relief package in 2020 (Box 3.3).

Box 3.3   Free Cooking Gas Cylinders under Pradhan Mantri Ujjwala Yojana

The Pradhan Mantri Ujjwala Yojana was launched in 2016 to provide subsidized liquefied petroleum gas (LPG) to households without cooking gas connections. These household were using traditional cooking fuels such as firewood, coal and cow dung cakes, which had a detrimental impact on women's health as well as environment. The government scheme encouraged the use of LPG connections to improve social and health conditions of women, as several studies had indicated that clean fuel offered major health benefits for homemakers through a perceptible improvement in household air quality. Given that household financial decisions were mostly made by men, the studies indicated that the adoption of LPG might be more widespread with direct subsidies to women. Under the scheme, the government directly transferred sufficient funds to purchase an LPG cylinder to the accounts of eligible women. Along with their deposit-free connections, the beneficiaries were also provided a stove (hotplate) and funds for a free cylinder refill.

Initially, the scheme targeted 80 million households—a target that was achieved in September 2019. In August 2021, "Ujjwala 2.0" was launched to benefit another 10 million low-income households that were not covered in the earlier phase. The focus of this round was on reaching migrants, including those living and working outside their domicile states without access to valid proof-of-address and people residing in forests, islands, and tea gardens.

Source: Asian Development Bank team analysis based on Government of India, https://www.pmuy.gov.in/.

ADB provided TA for carrying out an impact evaluation of the scheme's performance among beneficiary households across eight states. The study found that 100% of beneficiary households from the sample had PMUY-supplied LPG.[12] However, only 21% of them used LPG on a sustained basis. The study found that higher use of LPG was linked to higher levels of education, as well as higher incomes and more spending power among beneficiaries and nonbeneficiaries.

The study suggested the possibility that PMUY benefits make more economic sense for households with sufficient earning potential. Consequently, free or subsidized cylinders and refills and doorstep delivery are crucial to sustain LPG usage among households with lower earnings. The ADB study attributed the scheme's lower adoption in rural areas to cylinder cost, additional transport expenses, and behavioral and cultural underpinnings. The findings of the ADB study and its recommendations will help the government better design campaigns to help more households to transition to clean fuel, plug identified gaps in the sustainability of the scheme, and improve future implementation.

---

[11] The study interviewed over 1,311 migrants and 450 nonmigrants and 166 FPS dealers, in addition to over 50 government and other relevant stakeholders at the national and state levels.

[12] Sample included 7,003 rural and 1,470 urban households.

Grant for Emergency Procurement of Thermal Scanners

As the global movement of people came to a complete halt with the lockdown in March 2020, many Indians were stranded abroad and needed to urgently return to their homes and families. Thus, targeted testing was needed to facilitate the movement of people through ports of entry (POEs). Mass thermal screening (MTS) systems were an ideal solution to achieve efficient screening at POEs, while also maintaining appropriate social distancing.

ADB directed $0.5 million from its ongoing $3 million regional TA for India to support the procurement and delivery of 10 MTS systems for the screening of large numbers of passengers at international airports. By June 2020, UNICEF, as the partner agency, actively commissioned and installed the MTS systems in coordination with MOHFW and facilitated the training of 35 airport staff members on their operation. This achievement presented a suitable backdrop to expand assistance to fund, procure, and deploy 62 additional MTS systems. This was funded through another $3 million ADB grant (Box 3.4).

Box 3.4   Procuring and Deploying Mass Thermal Scanners

Objective

To further ramp up the country's capacity to screen at international airports and seaports, ADB facilitated $3 million in grant support via the Asia Pacific Disaster Response Fund—with the Government of Japan as its major contributor—to purchase additional mass thermal screening (MTS) systems. ADB again partnered with United Nations Children's Fund (UNICEF) in India to procure and install the 62 scanners across 27 airports and 9 seaports and to train an additional 125 key staff to operate the MTS systems.

"This support will enhance disease surveillance and help in early detection, contact tracing, and treatment. This will be further supplemented by other public health measures."

—Sungsup Ra, Director, Human and Social Development, South Asia, ADB

Output

Of the 62 MTS systems, 53 were commissioned without any major delays. However, nine scanners across seven sites faced delays due to pending work at the installation site, the subsequent change from an originally identified site to a new one, or ongoing work at the port of entry (POE). Ultimately, 61 MTS systems were installed at 26 international airports and nine seaports by November 2021, with the final installation at Lucknow International Airport occurring in 2022.

A thermal scanner installed at Indira Gandhi International Airport, New Delhi (photo courtesy UNICEF).

continued on next page

Outcomes

The MTS systems provided vital support in the quick and accurate detection of fever for early coronavirus disease (COVID-19) identification at POEs. Monitoring by UNICEF at several sites found the systems to be fully functional and well utilized. The ADB grant proved to be an excellent solution for swift case identification at POEs, allowing for more focused testing only for those with symptoms, which was central to the Government of India's containment plan for COVID-19.

With the coordination and concurrence of both ADB and the government, savings under the grant were redeployed by UNICEF to procure five RT-PCR machines, which were installed at five sites identified by the Ministry of Health and Family Welfare across north, and northeast India.

RT-PCR = Real-time reverse transcriptase-polymerase chain reaction.

Source: UNICEF, India. https://www.unicef.org/india/stories/adb-unicef-install-61-new-thermal-scanners-screening-passengers-ports-and-airports-0.

Impact of the CARES Plus Program

As mentioned earlier, the CPRO loan, in tandem with the TA and grant, formed a package of assistance collectively known as CARES Plus. It was timely, targeted, and temporary—the "three Ts" that characterize a good stimulus package.[13] CARES Plus filled critical financial and technical gaps in India's COVID-19 response and helped deliver health and social protection to vulnerable sections when most needed (Box 3.5).

Box 3.5   Achievements of CARES Plus

CARES Plus achieved the following:

1. Established dedicated COVID-19 health facilities and catalyzed the exponential growth of health infrastructure in the country, including operationalizing new testing and diagnostic labs, to improve access and shorten testing times.
2. Created an improved IT-based unified health surveillance system that strengthened evidence-based responses.[a]
3. Ramped up the capacities of emergency health facilities, increased the number of workers in the health care sector, strengthened workforce capacity, scaled up research to identify new pathogens, and deployed new medical technologies.
4. Supported the government's short-term fiscal responses at the macroeconomic level and financed urgent measures including food, fuel, and cash transfers to offset the economic hardships faced by poor people during the initial stages of the pandemic.
5. Assisted the stated purpose of the government's COVID-19 response efficiently, with guidance from the Department of Economic Affairs and close coordination with other ministries of the government. The CPRO instrument helped mobilize resources efficiently by securing and administering program funds, ensuring a rapid response to government requests.

COVID-19 = coronavirus disease, CPRO = COVID-19 Pandemic Response Option, IT = information technology.

[a] Source: Indian Council of Medical Research

Source: Asian Development Bank.

Timely ADB assistance under the program was critical in ensuring speedy implementation of the government's response measures, potentially averting socioeconomic distress to millions of people. Close coordination between ADB and DEA as well as ADB's fast-tracked business processes helped develop the program in a timely manner. The "One ADB" approach enabled speedy inputs and needed expertise through effective design of

[13]   European Central Bank. 2009. Box 7: The Effectiveness of Various Fiscal Measures to Stimulate the Economy. *Monthly Bulletin.* March 2009. Frankfurt. p. 78.

the program's emergency operations. Periodic collation of program data validating the design and monitoring framework results chain was also instrumental in efficient and timely monitoring of the program's impact.

By supporting increased expenditure, the program played a vital role in ensuring the government's ability to continue its routine social welfare programs alongside pandemic relief measures. The success of the program and associated TA resulted in the government extending its key COVID-19 response actions and support until late 2022, resulting in the following additional achievements:

(i)   Insurance coverage for health workers and accredited social health activists, initially valid until 30 June 2020, was extended periodically till October 2022.

(ii)   Originally a 3-month program, the allocation of free wheat, rice, and pulses under PMGKY for vulnerable groups, including women-led households, was extended till November 2020.[14] It was restarted during the second wave of the pandemic in May 2021 and received multiple extensions until the end of 2022.[15]

(iii) The free LPG cylinder scheme, initially announced for April–June 2020, was extended until December 2020 to ameliorate the impact of the pandemic lockdowns for poor and vulnerable sections of the population.

CARES Plus served health care and social protection objectives throughout 2020–2021, while the extensions beyond the originally conceived period contributed to the initial stages of India's post-pandemic recovery in 2022. In January 2023, the government adopted the free rations facility under Pradhan Mantri Garib Kalyan Ann Yojana as the new overarching scheme to benefit 800 million priority households and Antyodaya Anna Yojana beneficiaries, as per entitlement under the National Food Security Act, 2023.[16]

Strengthening Public Health Systems for Equitable Access and Future Pandemic Preparedness

The pandemic severely tested India's health care system. Urban areas, which were especially vulnerable to the spread of communicable diseases, were severely impacted by the virus' spread (Box 3.6). The first nationwide sero-survey for COVID-19 indicated a 1.89 times higher risk of spread in urban informal settlements as compared to rural areas.[17] A WHO Situation Update Report on COVID-19 released in March 2020 also pointed to a concentration of 35% of all cases in India in 20 urban agglomerations.[18] During the pandemic, management of

14   Extensions to the PMGKAY were announced on 1 July 2020 and 28 September 2020. | Government of India, Ministry of Consumer Affairs, Food & Public Distribution. 2020. Estimated cost for distribution of foodgrains (Rice and Wheat) and pulses under Pradhan Mantri Garib Kalyan Ann Yojana during April – November 2020 is around Rs 1,48,938 crore. Press release through the Press Information Bureau. 1 July. https://pib.gov.in/PressReleasePage.aspx?PRID=1635678. | Government of India, Ministry of Consumer Affairs, Food & Public Distribution. 2022. Centre extends Pradhan Mantri Garib Kalyan Ann Yojana (PMGKAY) for another three months (October 2022-December 2022). Press release through the Press Information Bureau. 28 September. https://pib.gov.in/PressReleasePage.aspx?PRID=1862945.

15   ENS Economic Bureau. 2022. IMF working paper: 'In pandemic, food subsidy kept extreme poverty low'. *Indian Express.* 7 April. https://indianexpress.com/article/india/pmgkay-food-subsidy-free-foodgrains-coronavirus-7856979/. | T. Ramakrishnan. 2022. Weighing in on PMGKAY, the free grains scheme. *The Hindu.* 18 November. https://www.thehindu.com/opinion/op-ed/weighing-in-on-pmgkay-the-free-grains-scheme/article66149854.ece.

16   Government of India, Ministry of Consumer Affairs, Food & Public Distribution. 2023. Centre names new integrated food security scheme launched from 1 January 2023 as "Pradhan Mantri Garib Kalyan Ann Yojana (PMGKAY). Press release through the Press Information Bureau. 11 January. https://pib.gov.in/PressReleasePage.aspx?PRID=1890272.

17   Government of India, Ministry of Health and Family Welfare. 2020. Updates on COVID-19. Press release through the Press Information Bureau. 11 June. https://pib.gov.in/PressReleasePage.aspx?PRID=1630922.

18   World Health Organization. 2020. Novel Coronavirus Disease (COVID-19) Situation Update Report – 35. New Delhi. https://www.who.int/docs/default-source/wrindia/situation-report/india-situation-report-35.pdf.

Box 3.6   Pre-Pandemic Urban Health Indicators in India

The National Family Health Survey-4 (NFHS-4) conducted in 2015–2016 identified much scope for improvement in health indicators for urban areas. Growth in the urban population, which stood at 461 million in 2018, outpaced the capacity of most Indian cities to provide basic social services. Further, the country's urban population is projected to reach 877 million by 2050.[a] Contrary to the common perception, health indicators of the urban poor are often worse than for their rural counterparts in India despite a large presence of private sector providers.

An analysis of NFHS-4 data (undertaken by the International Institute of Population Science, Mumbai) found the complete immunization of 57.7% of urban poor children (aged 12–23 months) versus 61.3% for rural poor children. An estimated 62.7% of urban poor children were found to be suffering from anemia against 59.5% for rural poor children. The survey data also revealed poor uptake of preventive health examinations—cervical (20%), breast (9.3%), and oral cavity (10.3%)—by urban poor women (aged 15–49 years). Vulnerability to communicable and vector-borne diseases and the incidence of noncommunicable diseases were also higher among poor people living in congested urban areas.

[a] United Nations Department of Economic and Social Affairs. 2018. *Revision of World Urbanization Prospects*. New York. https://www.un.org/en/desa/2018-revision-world-urbanization-prospects.

Source: Asian Development Bank.

health emergencies and ensuring health sector responsiveness was a challenge not just for COVID-19 cases but also for noncommunicable diseases (NCDs) such as diabetes, hypertension, and cancer, and other health conditions including pregnancies and emergencies.

Aware of the challenge and looking into the gaps revealed in the health systems during COVID-19, the Government of India launched the Pradhan Mantri Ayushman Bharat Health Infrastructure Mission (PM-ABHIM) on 25 October 2021. The objective was to strengthen public health systems to prepare for future pandemics and other emergencies by addressing the gaps revealed by the pandemic with expansion of quality health services. Building on its past support to National Urban Health Mission that assisted in strengthening response to the pandemic in urban areas (Box 3.7), ADB approved a $300 million results-based loan program—Strengthening Comprehensive Primary Health Care in Urban Areas under PM-ABHIM.

Box 3.7   ADB's Past Support to Improve Urban Health Care Delivery in India

To strengthen urban public health systems, ADB supported the National Urban Health Mission (NUHM) with a $300 million results-based loan in 2015–2016.[a] Key achievements included the operationalization of 4,500 urban primary health centers and improved availability of outreach services through the onboarding of more than 30,000 accredited social health activists, who are women community volunteers, to serve in urban vulnerable pockets. From 2014 to 2019, the NUHM increased the share of institutional deliveries from 53.1% to 72.1% and raised completed immunization rates for children aged 1 year and below from 49.6% to 64.7%. The project was also supported by a $3.8 million technical assistance to assist state-level institutional capacity assessments, monitor results, and promote innovations in urban health. The assistance also supported the rollout of comprehensive primary health care through health and wellness centers in urban areas.

[a] ADB. 2015. *Report and Recommendation of the President to the Board of Directors: Proposed Results-Based Loan and Administration of Technical Assistance Grant to India for Supporting National Urban Health Mission*. Manila.

Objective

The program aimed to improve access to quality health services by poor and vulnerable populations in urban informal settlements in select states. This was to be done through expansion of quality health care services in urban primary health centers (UPHCs) and health and wellness centers (HWCs). As of November 2020, these states together accounted for 65% of India's urban population, 78% of its urban informal settlement dwellers, and 71% of its functional UPHCs. At the same time, these states also accounted for 73% of confirmed COVID-19 cases and 77% of all deaths from COVID-19.

The ADB-funded program supports the objectives of Ayushman Bharat HWCs and PM-ABHIM with a strong focus on the COVID-19 pandemic response and health system resilience across 13 select states.[19] With an overarching goal of achieving universal health coverage in urban areas, ADB support is expected to benefit 256 million urban Indians from 2021 to 2024, of which, 51 million live in informal settlements. Drawing from previous support to the National Urban Health Mission, ADB focused on setting meaningful gender targets; introducing outcome-level, disbursement-linked indicators under direct control of the program; and independently verifying impacts of the results-based loan.

Outputs

The program dealt with strengthening comprehensive primary health care services in urban areas, including operationalizing HWCs, enhancing facilities for the screening of NCDs, and improving the availability of essential medicines (Figure 3.3).

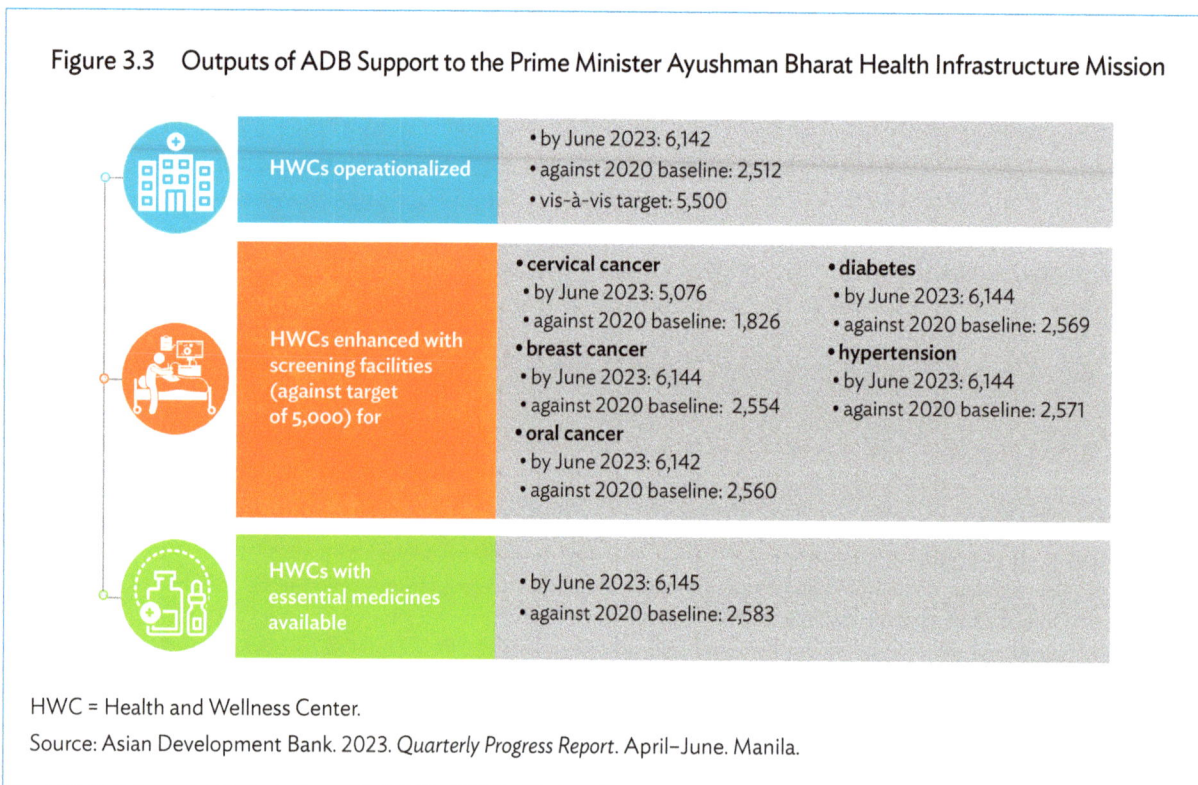

Figure 3.3   Outputs of ADB Support to the Prime Minister Ayushman Bharat Health Infrastructure Mission

HWCs operationalized
- by June 2023: 6,142
- against 2020 baseline: 2,512
- vis-à-vis target: 5,500

HWCs enhanced with screening facilities (against target of 5,000) for
- cervical cancer
  - by June 2023: 5,076
  - against 2020 baseline: 1,826
- breast cancer
  - by June 2023: 6,144
  - against 2020 baseline: 2,554
- oral cancer
  - by June 2023: 6,142
  - against 2020 baseline: 2,560
- diabetes
  - by June 2023: 6,144
  - against 2020 baseline: 2,569
- hypertension
  - by June 2023: 6,144
  - against 2020 baseline: 2,571

HWCs with essential medicines available
- by June 2023: 6,145
- against 2020 baseline: 2,583

HWC = Health and Wellness Center.
Source: Asian Development Bank. 2023. *Quarterly Progress Report*. April–June. Manila.

---

[19]   Andhra Pradesh, Assam, Chhattisgarh, Gujarat, Haryana, Jharkhand, Karnataka, Madhya Pradesh, Maharashtra, Rajasthan, Tamil Nadu, Telangana, and West Bengal.

Outcomes

The program outcomes, which are proposed to be achieved by 2025, are aligned with the objective of universal access to good quality health care services set forth in the National Health Policy, 2017.[20] The quarterly progress report points to substantial improvements in the utilization of the HWCs in terms of footfalls, screenings for NCDs, and improvements in women health care (Figure 3.4).

Figure 3.4   Outcomes of ADB Support to the Prime Minister Ayushman Bharat Health Infrastructure Mission

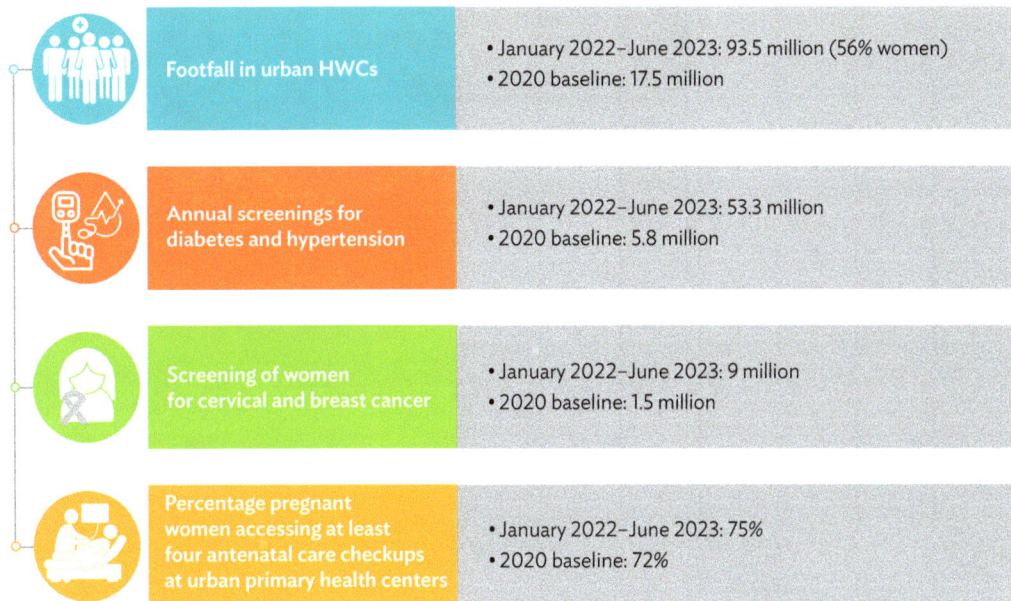

	Footfall in urban HWCs	• January 2022–June 2023: 93.5 million (56% women) • 2020 baseline: 17.5 million
	Annual screenings for diabetes and hypertension	• January 2022–June 2023: 53.3 million • 2020 baseline: 5.8 million
	Screening of women for cervical and breast cancer	• January 2022–June 2023: 9 million • 2020 baseline: 1.5 million
	Percentage pregnant women accessing at least four antenatal care checkups at urban primary health centers	• January 2022–June 2023: 75% • 2020 baseline: 72%

HWC = health and wellness center.
Source: Asian Development Bank.

Impact

The ADB-supported program is on course to expand access to an increased range of medical services through UPHCs and HWCs. Such access was crucial during the COVID-19 pandemic and going forward, it will equip the health care system to better respond to future health crises (Box 3.8).

---

20   Government of India, Ministry of Health and Family Welfare. 2017. *National Health Policy 2017*. New Delhi. https://main.mohfw.gov.in/sites/default/files/9147562941489753121.pdf.

Box 3.8   Primary Health Care Services Get a Boost in Gandhinagar, Gujarat

The urban primary health center (UPHC) in Gandhinagar, Gujarat, is one where a range of services have been upgraded under the ADB-funded Strengthening Comprehensive Primary Health Care in Urban Areas Program under Pradhan Mantri Ayushman Bharat Health Infrastructure Mission. Since the upgrading of services, the UPHC has witnessed increased visits from patients, including women. It has enhanced facilities for the testing and vaccination of children and improved access to specialist health services, including private sector specialists.

UPHC Gandhinagar, Gujarat figures among health centers upgraded with comprehensive primary health care services.

Rohit Kalsariya, a medical officer at the UPHC says, "We are increasingly handling patients with noncommunicable diseases such as diabetes, hypertension, and cervical and breast cancer. The center also offers prenatal care besides handling common illnesses such as flu, malaria, anemia, cough, cold etc...A team of private health care professionals, including a gynecologist, pediatrician, ophthalmologist, and orthopedic surgeon, visit the hospital once a week."

Rohit Kalsariya attending to patients at the UPHC, Gandhinagar, Gujarat.

Another program objective is to facilitate management of urban health centers by local urban bodies, which UPHC Gandhinagar has achieved.

"We have seen that infrastructure has gradually improved, and facilities are better now since the center has been brought under the control of the Municipal Corporation, Gandhinagar," says Kalsariya.

Source: Asian Development Bank.

Looking Ahead

The PM-ABHIM has the potential to significantly strengthen India's urban health system through upgraded UPHCs and HWCs. The behavior change campaigns and outreach efforts are raising awareness of modern health care to promote the utilization of these centers by urban dwellers, especially women and other vulnerable groups, beyond the most common ailments. By 2024, ADB's Strengthening Comprehensive Primary Health Care in Urban Areas Program under PM-ABHIM is expected to achieve its remaining outcomes of creating crucial infrastructure for delivering quality primary care in urban areas. This will lead to a noticeable difference in health outcomes in urban areas, especially in the context of continuing to deliver health services for major ailments such as cancer and other NCDs, and ensure better preparedness for unforeseen health emergencies such as the COVID-19 pandemic.

4 Controlling the Contagion: ADB Assistance in Rolling Out and Ramping Up the COVID-19 Vaccination Drive in India

India's initial strategy to deal with COVID-19 focused on containment and a relief package to provide immediate help to the poor and vulnerable population. The next phase focused on controlling the contagion through vaccines that would help save lives, ease pressure on the health care system, and pave the way for a return to normalcy. Equitable access to safe and effective vaccines was critical to ending the pandemic. Throughout 2020, there were no known cures, available vaccines, or proven remedies to deal with COVID-19. Social distancing and prevention control protocols were the only means to contain the virus' spread.

By January 2021, the first vaccine candidates emerged that were cleared for emergency use. India launched a COVID-19 vaccination campaign on 16 January 2021 that turned out to be the world's biggest inoculation drive. The second COVID-19 wave in April–May 2021 stretched India's health care system and infrastructure to the limits, which prompted the government to rapidly expand vaccination coverage to a larger share of the population. By June 2021, quickly vaccinating the entire population was the immediate task at hand and ADB support would be critical for achieving this.

Health care workers celebrate the rollout of the first phase of the vaccination drive at a Delhi hospital (photo courtesy Press Information Bureau, Government of India).

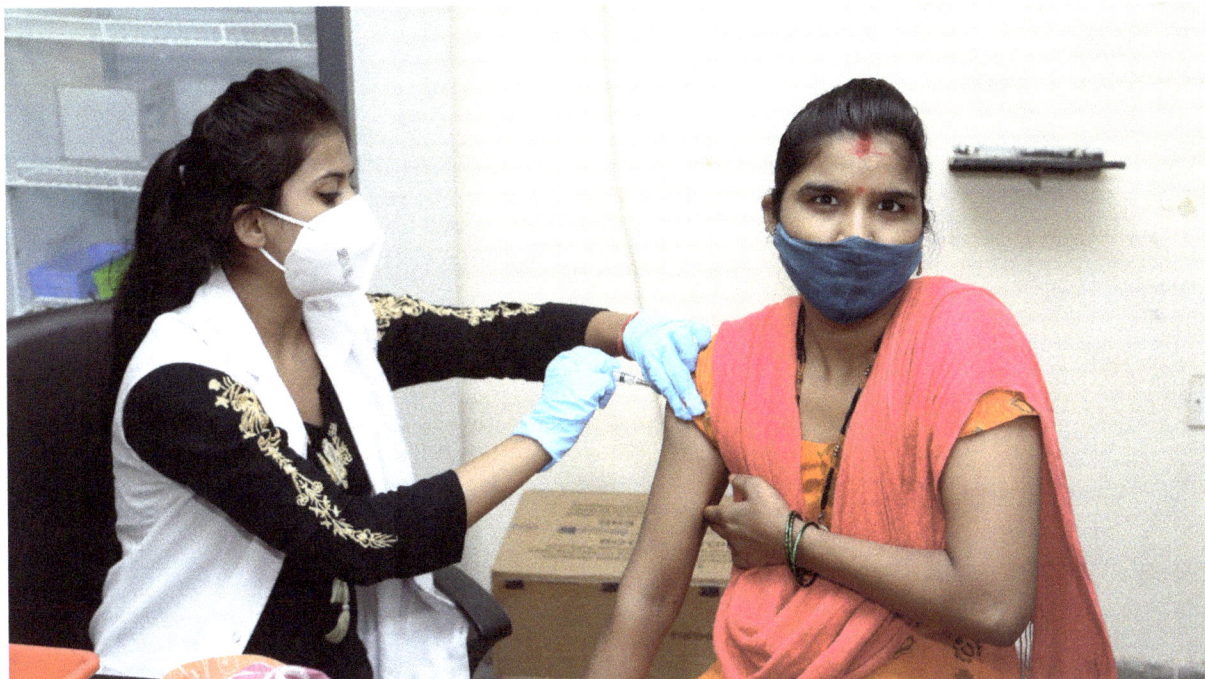

Sita, a daily wage worker, getting vaccinated at a government health center in Basant Gaon in Delhi.

India's vaccination campaign, launched in January 2021, was targeted to cover health care and other frontline workers involved in essential services. In early March 2021, the emergency-use license was expanded to the 60 plus population and those over 45 years old with co-morbidities. In April 2021, the country suffered a devastating second wave, registering 400,000 new cases daily by early May 2021.[21] Given the second wave and the possible threat of a third wave, the government reevaluated its vaccine strategy and expanded it to inoculate every Indian above the age of 18 years (944 million individuals) by September 2021. An estimated 2 billion doses would be needed to achieve this. ADB would provide the government with the immediate financial support it needed to procure eligible vaccines to inoculate its target population and limit the adverse impacts of the pandemic.

Objective of ADB Support to India's COVID-19 Vaccination Drive

To help meet the government's huge financing requirements for procuring vaccines, ADB approved the $1.5 billion Responsive COVID-19 Vaccines for Recovery Project. The financing was drawn from ADB's Asia Pacific Vaccine Access Facility (APVAX) for DMCs.[22] The Asian Infrastructure Investment Bank co-financed the effort. ADB assistance aimed to administer 667 million doses to 317 million people across India by 2024. Of the total targeted population, 47.5% were women. Support to the vaccination program was intended to accelerate India's overall health, social, and economic recovery from COVID-19.

---

[21]   R. Sood, K. Kapur, and O.C. Kurian. 2021. India's Vaccine Rollout: A Reality Check, Special Report no. 139. https://www.orfonline.org/wp-content/uploads/2021/05/ORF_SpecialReport_139_Vaccination_FinalForUpload.pdf.

[22]   ADB. 2020. ADB's Support to Enhance COVID-19 Vaccine Access. Manila. https://www.adb.org/sites/default/files/institutional-document/662801/adb-support-covid-19-vaccine-access.pdf.

Output of ADB Support to India's COVID-19 Vaccination Drive

By December 2022, an aggregate of 2.1 billion vaccine doses—981.8 million first doses, 910.7 million second doses, and 213.8 million precaution (or booster) doses—had been administered across all project states. Of this, reimbursement for 526.5 million doses was delivered to participating states under ADB's APVAX facility, with the project effectively delivering vaccines at a cost of $3 per dose (Figure 4.1).

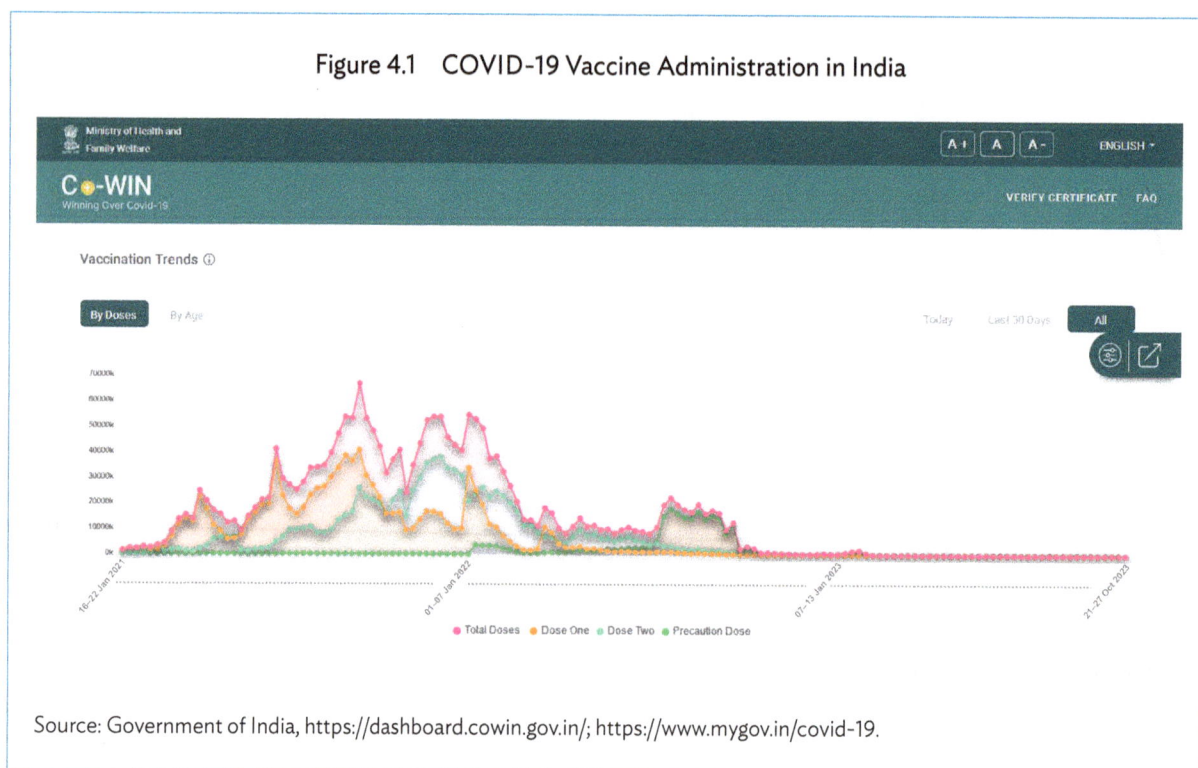

Figure 4.1   COVID-19 Vaccine Administration in India

Source: Government of India, https://dashboard.cowin.gov.in/; https://www.mygov.in/covid-19.

To facilitate vaccination delivery, the government and development partners made available adequate resources and identified a network of COVID-19 vaccination centers (CVCs) across the country. This was complemented by effective campaigns to increase willingness for vaccination among priority populations. By location, 70.9% doses were administered at rural CVCs, 28.7% at urban CVCs, and the rest at CVCs identified as neither urban nor rural.

ADB's assistance ensured effective procurement and delivery of vaccines to target populations. The entire effort was undertaken in coordination with other development partners to ensure an inclusive COVID-19 vaccination campaign. For example, UNICEF's Risk Communication and Community Engagement (RCCE) was one such joint intervention with ADB that assisted in the vaccination of people in rural areas and marginalized groups in urban informal settlements. Under the RCCE, a total of 151,000 persons, including 97,000 women, received face-to-face information on challenges pertaining to the uptake of a second dose of the COVID-19 vaccine, and 802 village-level meetings were organized.

As part of the awareness campaign for this UNICEF initiative, ADB helped organize 11 online sessions and 135 district-level meetings across 11 states—totaling 2,526 person-days of beneficiary participation (of which 61% were women)—on social security schemes, Ayushman Bharat, and other relevant state-level health schemes. ADB's outreach led to the orientation of over 2,880 tribal leaders and influencers, the organizing of 734 awareness meetings for village chiefs to mobilize villagers for full vaccine coverage at camps, and capacity building among medical professionals on COVID-19-sensitive behavior for teenagers.

Storing and transporting vaccines at low temperature was a challenge that required cold-chain capacity across the country. Yet, unstable electricity supplies and power disruptions posed a major challenge in rural and remote areas. To overcome this challenge, ADB in partnership with UNICEF, supported the installation of solar direct drives in primary health centers. Provided by the Government of Japan, these solar direct drives helped to significantly reduce travel times for vaccine teams, thus improving access and efficiency while speeding up the vaccination drive to benefit remote and vulnerable groups.

Outcomes of ADB Support to India's COVID-19 Vaccination Drive

ADB assistance helped expand vaccine coverage in several Indian states. Of a total of 2.1 billion COVID-19 vaccine doses, 1.03 billion (49.1%) were administered to women through 31 December 2022, against a target share of at least 47.5% for women. While urban areas were easier to cover due to their more developed cold-chain vaccine logistics, the disproportionately large share of doses administered at CVCs in rural areas (70.9%) positively affected overall coverage. To maximize reach and impact, the goverment launched innovative citizen-friendly initiatives such as Har Ghar Dastak (A Knock on Every Door), workplace and close-to-home CVCs, school-based vaccination drives, the vaccination of persons with no identity documents, and mobile vaccination teams.

Covering all vulnerable groups, India administered a billion vaccine doses by October 2021 and doubled it within the next 9 months. ADB assistance helped boost government's efforts to procure, distribute, and administer COVID-19 vaccines and meet the targeted geographic and gender equity outputs and outcomes.[23] Regular reviews with states and Union Territories were undertaken to share best practices for effective implementation of India's COVID-19 vaccination program. On 31 January 2023, ADB convened a best practices conclave to disseminate lessons learned from the vaccine drive, with a focus on gender equality and social inclusion, to strengthen systems for future pandemic response.

To understand the prevailing myths among the urban poor on getting themselves vaccinated, and to create awareness among them on the utility of the vaccine, ADB supported multicentric studies.[24] The observations were shared with the health authorities and published, too, for wider dissemination.

---

[23]   Government of India. Ministry of Health and Family Welfare. 2022. India achieves major landmark of '200 Crore' COVID-19 Vaccinations. Press release through the Press Information Bureau of India. 17 July. https://pib.gov.in/PressReleasePage.aspx?PRID=1842157.,

[24]   S. Tamysetty et al. 2021. Predictors of COVID-19 Vaccine Confidence: Findings from Slums of Four Major Metro Cities of India. *Vaccines (Basel)*. 31 December; 10(1): 60.

Impact of India's COVID-19 Vaccination Drive

The vaccination program slowed the virus' transmission and reduced the susceptibility of millions of Indians to COVID-19, which gradually eased the hardships of the pandemic beginning in the second half of 2021. ADB's support to UNICEF's RCCE also helped additionally vaccinate several hundred thousand individuals and fostered greater awareness of COVID-19 symptoms (e.g., sore throat, fever, and shortness of breath) and appropriate behavior to deal with contracting the virus (e.g., consulting a physician and the proper wearing and disposal of masks). Underscoring the success of these COVID-19 outreach activities, a midline survey assessment indicated an increase in the proportion of households who believed the government's appropriate behavior messages would continue to motivate people. The findings also pointed to improvements in knowledge about the management of COVID-19 among surveyed households and reduced misgivings about the vaccine and its safety for pregnant and lactating women and children.

Looking Ahead

ADB is continuing to undertake studies to understand various aspects of vaccine uptake and the campaign's impact on gender equality and social inclusion. In addition, a study is being conducted by Tata Institute of Social Sciences, Mumbai, in six states to identify social, behavioral, demographic, geographic, and other determinants of vaccine uptake. Inferences from the endline survey with regard to social behavior changes in managing COVID-19 and implementing vaccination campaigns will be available by the end of 2023 to help shape ADB support to future responses.

5 ADB Support to the Private Sector during the Pandemic

Tapping the Private Sector to Strengthen India's Fight against the Pandemic

The spread of the pandemic stretched India's public sector health care facilities. The involvement of the private sector helped the central and state governments meet this challenge in combating the infectious disease. To supplement government efforts to manage COVID-19, ADB provided funding support to scale up the private sector's critical care facilities and augment the national response to the pandemic (Box 5.1).

Box 5.1   Global Health Private Limited COVID-19 Hospital Service Delivery Project

Overview

Hospitals and health care service providers were tested to the limit through most of 2020–2021, and augmenting their capabilities was a continuous challenge. The private sector is a significant source of health care, particularly in urban areas across India. The COVID-19 pandemic spawned a sudden spurt in demand for critical health care equipment, facilities, and workforce in medical, diagnostic, paramedical, auxiliary, treatment, and disposal facility staff. The additional challenge was to contain the spread of the contagion among health care staff while caring for infected patients which required hospitals to put in place stringent safety protocols. Even large private health care institutions felt the pressure of dealing with the unexpected pandemic load while being required to incur additional capital expenditures on critical life support equipment such as ventilators.

Global Health Private Limited (GHPL) is one of the largest private, multispecialty tertiary care providers in India's North and East regions, operating five hospitals (with 2,571 installed beds) and four clinics under the brand "Medanta" as of December 2022.

Following the COVID-19 pandemic outbreak in early 2020, GHPL anticipated the challenge of declining revenues and increased expenses as people avoided hospitals except for acute emergencies while hospitals would bear additional costs in order to comply with the pandemic protocols. With this scenario looming, GHPL approached ADB for assistance in March 2020. The ADB team moved quickly to get approval in August 2020 for a 3-year debt financing of up to $20 million to enable GHPL to operate fully and provide much-needed COVID-19 health services.

Objective

As a premier health care company, GHPL had the capacity to treat COVID-19 patients in its isolation wards and critical care units in Gurugram, Indore, Ranchi, and Lucknow. However, with the pandemic spreading fast, its Medanta hospitals needed to ramp up their emergency care capacity. The objective of ADB assistance was to help GHPL improve its hospital service delivery and meet short- and medium-term funding needs exacerbated by the pandemic.

continued on next page

Box 5.1 *continued*

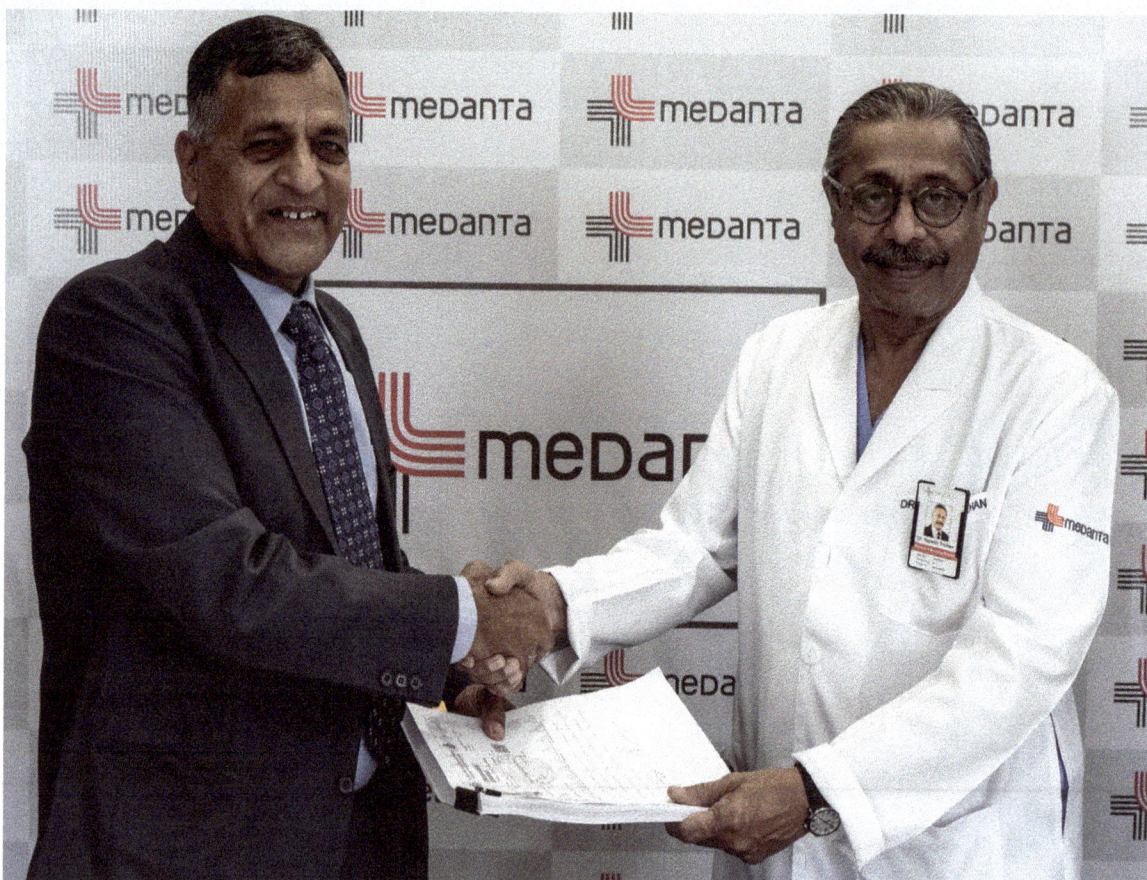

ADB extended funding support to Global Health Private Limited to help improve its hospital service delivery during the pandemic.

Outputs

The ADB assistance helped Medanta hospitals build up their critical care capacity to prepare for the expected rise in COVID-19 cases. The financing supported purchase of essential patient care equipment, personal protective equipment, and basic hygiene products; trained staff for infection prevention and control; and ensured the continued provision of essential and nonessential health care services.

ADB disbursed $13.4 million to GHPL in May 2021 at the peak of the severe second wave of COVID-19 in India. The deadly wave of infections caused by the delta variant created widespread shortages of critical care equipment and intensive care capacities. However, Medanta was ready to deal with the pandemic surge after increasing bed capacity from 414 isolation beds in 2020 to 860 in 2021.

Outcomes

The project helped enhance the capacity of the private health system to respond to the public health emergency created by COVID-19. The working capital support to GHPL helped the health care provider meet its immediate financing needs to augment pandemic treatment, scale up staff trained in infection prevention, and purchase personal protective equipment. ADB's immediate response to GHPL with an early investment helped in containing COVID-19 and ramping up the private sector's healthcare capacity, which proved to be lifesaving.

continued on next page

Box 5.1   *continued*

Impact

ADB support helped to curtail the transmission of and morbidity and mortality due to COVID-19, in line with the Government of India's disease containment plan. The project's impacts aligned well with the key objective of ADB's pandemic response of enhancing the capacity of India's health system to respond to public health emergencies.

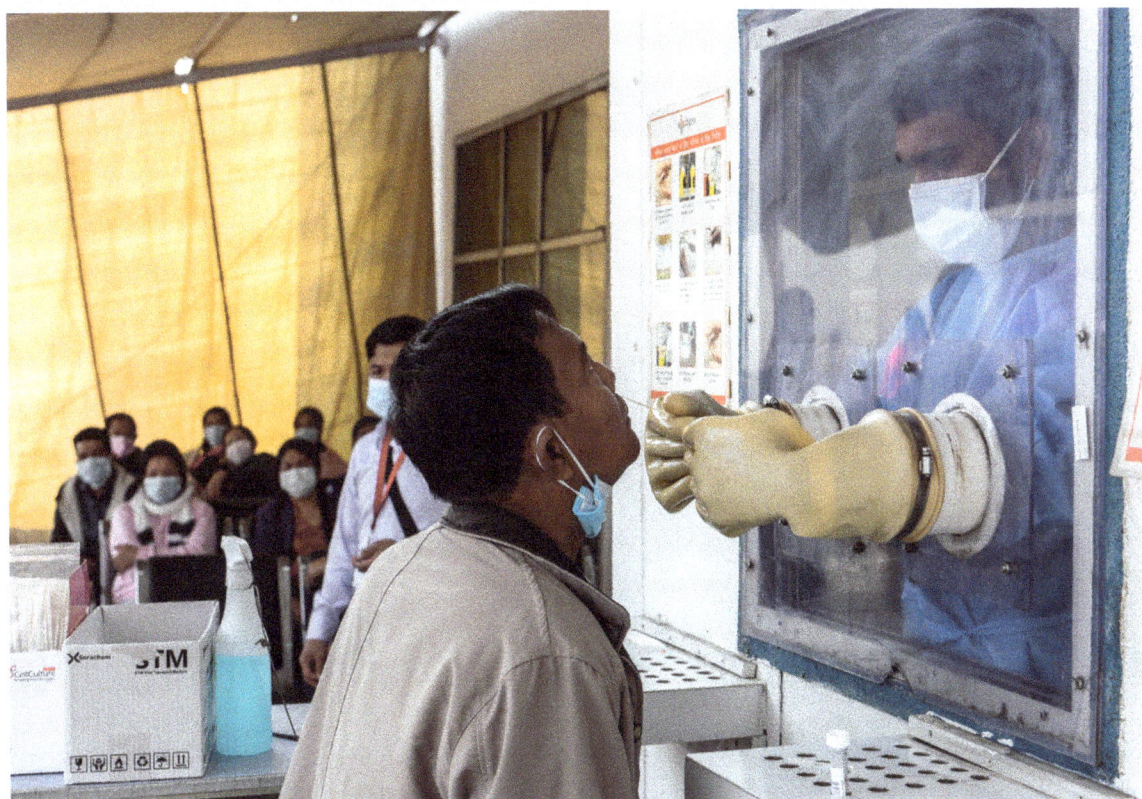

A lab technician taking nasal swab sample at Medanta Hospital in Gurugram, adjoining Delhi.

Source: Asian Development Bank

Immediate Support to Help Private Enterprises Sustain Operations

While the COVID-19 pandemic led to a huge loss of human life and presented an unprecedented challenge to public health, its economic consequences were equally devastating. Thousands of private enterprises faced an existential threat, putting the livelihoods of millions at risk.

During the pandemic-related lockdowns, daily business operations were halted to prevent transmission of the disease, causing severe disruption to many private businesses that needed to maintain their physical establishments, pay salaries, and keep supply chains going even as production and sales plummeted. Micro, small, and medium-sized enterprises (MSMEs) that lacked the financial resources or financing options of larger entities needed immediate support to continue incurring capital expenditures and withstand the many downside risks caused by the pandemic. In response to this initial phase of the pandemic, ADB offered nonsovereign commitments to provide much-needed liquidity support to private enterprises, including both large firms and MSMEs, helping to sustain their operations and maintain the livelihoods of their employees.

Debt Financing to Support Livelihoods—Suguna Foods

A. Overview of Suguna's Business Operations as the Pandemic Spread

In February–March 2020, poultry farms in India faced an abrupt demand contraction as rumors spread about the possibility of chickens being vectors of COVID-19. Furthermore, restrictions imposed on the movement of people and goods heavily impacted supplies. As a result, poultry prices fell drastically, leading to severe liquidity issues in the industry and putting the livelihoods of tens of thousands of contract farmers in jeopardy.

Suguna Foods Private Limited (Suguna) is one of the largest agribusiness companies in India and the largest producer of broiler chickens with a market share of 15%. In March 2020, Suguna employed more than 7,700 people and supported the livelihoods of 40,000 smallholder contractual poultry farmers, including 3,610 women farmers and 200,000 corn and soybean farmers. With such a large number of smallholders directly dependent on the value chain, Suguna had the same conundrum as other poultry businesses during the onset of COVID-19 in India.

Prior to the pandemic, Suguna had intended to expand its operations across multiple Indian states with modern feed mills, hatcheries, climate-controlled sheds, and meat processing lines. It had also sought to enlarge its smallholder poultry farmers' base to 55,000. To help Suguna's expansion, ADB had approved a capital expenditure (capex) loan of $25 million in March 2020 under the Inclusive Poultry Value Chain Project in India, as well as a TA for Gender Capacity Enhancement in Poultry.[25] However, the outbreak of the pandemic and subsequent lockdown prevented the loan from being executed. The demand shrinkage led to a severe liquidity crunch in Suguna, putting livelihoods at risk.

B. Objective

Suguna approached ADB for short-term financing assistance to tide over the pandemic-induced economic crisis. While the capex loan was on hold, Suguna's request was found suitable for ADB's COVID-19 emergency support based on the company's business model and structure, as well as its role in tackling India's nutrition challenges and promoting rural livelihoods. In June 2020, ADB financed Suguna with $10 million through senior, secured, nonconvertible debentures from its own resources for the Sustaining Poultry Farmer Income and Food Security Project. ADB's objective in supporting Suguna was to sustain rural livelihoods, promote gender inclusiveness, and expand nutrition security and food safety practices as part of a complete recovery from the pandemic.

C. Outputs

ADB's debt financing ensured payment to poultry farmers and feed suppliers; secured workers' livelihoods; enhanced gender equality in Suguna work environments; and increased the gender inclusiveness of Suguna's corporate social responsibility program. The disbursement of both tranches of the financing was completed by September 2020.[26] Support to farmers helped increase the number of women contract farmers from 3,610 to 3,845 during the first 2 years of the pandemic.

D. Outcomes

The ADB project promoted gender-inclusive rural livelihoods and reduced malnutrition by increasing production of affordable animal proteins.[27] ADB's liquidity support helped sustain the operations of 40,000 contract poultry farmers linked to Suguna's value chain and prevented the shutdown of India's largest broiler chicken producer (Box 5.2).

---

[25] ADB. 2020. *Report and Recommendation of the President to the Board of Directors: Proposed Loan and Technical Assistance to Suguna Foods Private Limited for the Inclusive Poultry Value Chain Project in India.* Manila. https://www.adb.org/sites/default/files/project-documents/53383/53383-001-rrp-en.pdf.

[26] The facility comprised three tranches, each up to $5 million. Two of three were disbursed on 29 April 2021 and 29 September 2021. Suguna did not avail Tranche 3 within the facility period, resulting in its expiry. https://www.adb.org/projects/54237-001/main.

[27] June 2020. ADB FAST Report. India. *Debt Financing Suguna Foods Private Limited Sustaining Poultry Farmer Income and Food Security Project.*

Box 5.2   ADB Assistance Helps Poultry Farmers to Stay in Business During the Pandemic

Mohammed Atiq, 27, who hails from Sitapur in the state of Uttar Pradesh, started contract poultry farming in 2017 after building a 5,400 square feet shed in 2017 on land owned by his family. Under the contract farming model, Suguna Foods Private Limited (Suguna Foods) has been supporting poultry farmers like Atiq with necessary inputs, including day-old chicks, feed, medicine and technical services. In return, farmers provide labor and nonmonetary capital such as land and farming sheds. Birds that reach slaughter weight are bought back by Suguna Foods and are either sold live via the wet market or processed as chicken meat. Farmers are paid per chicken at a fixed fee plus a performance bonus. This model ensures relatively predictable incomes for farmers.

ADB loan to Suguna Foods helped Mohammed Atiq to prevent further losses during COVID-19 lockdowns.

As his business prospered prior to 2020, Atiq bought an additional 6,000 square feet of land, mainly with the savings from his annual income of around ₹200,000 from poultry farming. However, when the pandemic struck, Atiq's poultry business was set back. Transport restrictions made it challenging to source feed for the birds. Atiq had to cull 4,000 birds to sustain his poultry operations. Further, false information associating chicken with the spread of COVID-19 contributed to the decline in poultry demand. This resulted in losses and tight liqidity conditions for Suguna Foods and its contract farmers.

With ADB financing, Suguna Foods bore most of the losses caused by the sharp decline in demand for poultry meat. Atiq said the Suguna Foods' assistance spared his business further losses, and allowed him to cover expenses.

"We are grateful to have received financial assistance from Suguna Foods to pay for essential costs," said Atiq. "While other companies in the industry struggled to keep their contract farmers, Suguna Foods did its best not to leave us. They gave us a minimum income during the crisis which enabled us to cover basic costs like electricity, something we could not have done without this financial help."

Source: Asian Development Bank.

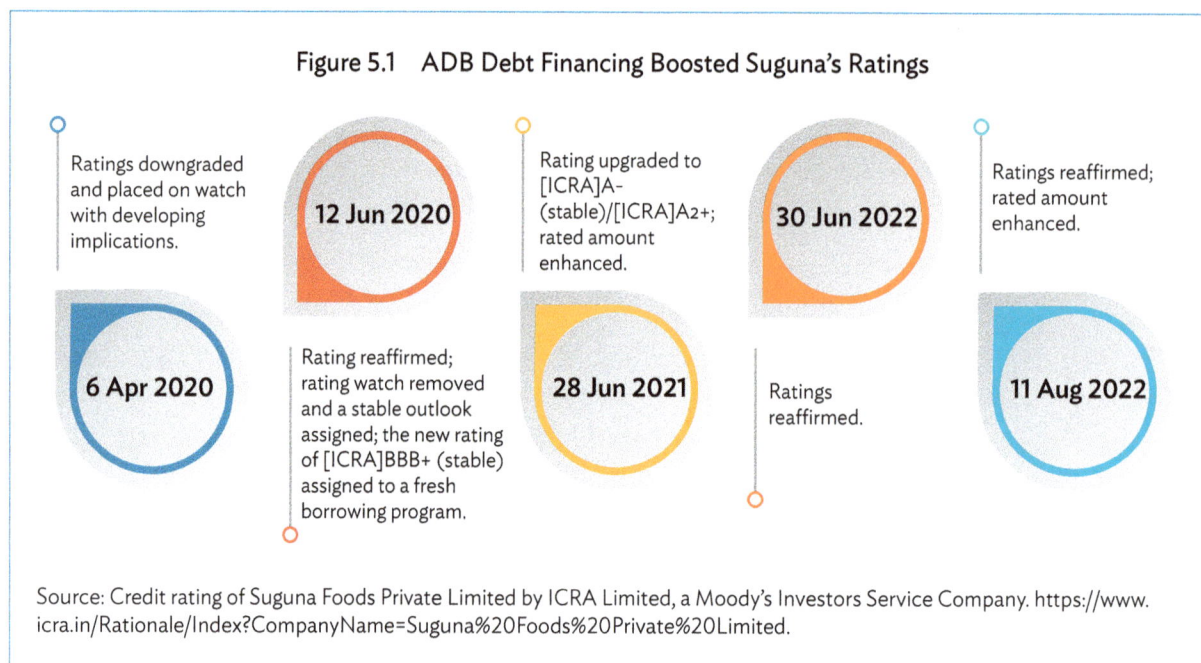

Figure 5.1   ADB Debt Financing Boosted Suguna's Ratings

6 Apr 2020 — Ratings downgraded and placed on watch with developing implications.

12 Jun 2020 — Rating reaffirmed; rating watch removed and a stable outlook assigned; the new rating of [ICRA]BBB+ (stable) assigned to a fresh borrowing program.

28 Jun 2021 — Rating upgraded to [ICRA]A- (stable)/[ICRA]A2+; rated amount enhanced.

30 Jun 2022 — Ratings reaffirmed.

11 Aug 2022 — Ratings reaffirmed; rated amount enhanced.

Source: Credit rating of Suguna Foods Private Limited by ICRA Limited, a Moody's Investors Service Company. https://www.icra.in/Rationale/Index?CompanyName=Suguna%20Foods%20Private%20Limited.

E.   Impact

The infused liquidity helped Suguna sustain its operations, retain its employees, and maintain the payments to the contract farmers. As demand for poultry recovered and grew steadily again after the economic shock of the initial months of the pandemic, Suguna strengthened its market position. Between March 2020 and December 2022, the company also successfully built inventory buffers and stabilized its operational parameters, resulting in revenue growth and improved margins, which eventually led to a credit ratings upgrade (following a downgrade at the onset of the pandemic) (Figure 5.1).

F.   Looking Ahead

ADB assistance to Suguna aligned to the government's long-term approach of strengthening the agriculture sector and improving farmers' incomes by plugging agricultural supply chain gaps, involving the private sector in development initiatives, and providing support to MSMEs. The assistance was also in line with India's National Action Plan for Egg and Poultry for raising farmers' incomes.

Liquidity Support to the Renewable Energy Sector—ReNew Power

The COVID-19 pandemic had a deep impact on the power sector globally through demand reductions, financial strains, and supply chain disruptions. With large commercial and industrial consumers reporting a precipitous drop in demand, already desperate power utilities in India were squeezed harder than ever. Plunging revenues, owing to weak demand and credit market disruptions caused by the lockdowns, damaged the liquidity profile of distribution companies in terms of debt service reserves and undrawn working capital limits, thereby increasing subsidy requirements and delaying payments to the power generation and transmission companies.

The renewable energy sector came under acute stress as solar and wind energy projects that were under construction faced labor shortages and delays in the supply of equipment and the acquisition of land. The installation of rooftop solar plants came to a halt. Even prior to the pandemic, weak power demand from commercial and industrial customers, high transmission and distribution losses, delayed payments from state-owned distribution companies, and lending bottlenecks had posed challenges for the renewable energy sector. The pandemic-induced lockdowns further worsened the situation.

A.   Overview

In a departure from the more common financing of capex, ADB identified working capital support as a key requirement of power producers during the pandemic. With this need in mind, ADB provided a debt financing facility of up to $50 million to ReNew Power Private Limited (RPPL) to partially finance its working capital needs that were exacerbated by lockdown-induced cash flow mismatches. Incorporated in 2011, RPPL (the largest independent renewable energy company in India) had 5.49 gigawatts of operational wind and solar power capacity across nine states in India as of 31 March 2020.

A majority of RPPL's operational portfolio (77.8%) consists of long-term power purchase agreements with distribution companies that have weak to moderate financial risk profiles. The lockdown was thus expected to extend receivable days for RPPL and increase its working capital cycle. This meant that it would need to provide greater working capital liquidity to its subsidiaries and affiliates at the same time its dividend income from subsidiaries and affiliates was declining.

The proceeds from the ADB debt financing facility were used by RPPL to fund its working capital requirements and infuse liquidity into operating special purpose vehicles (SPVs) via shareholder loans that enabled these SPVs to sustain business operations even with reduced cash flow (Box 5.3).

B.   Objective

The objective of ADB financing was to ensure that RPPL sustained operations and met its salary payment and other obligations during the COVID-19 pandemic. The facility also aimed to improve gender mainstreaming in both pandemic support measures for RPPL's staff and as part of its longer-term corporate social responsibility (CSR) measures. ADB's assistance was designed to complement the Government of India's efforts to ensure adequate liquidity in the financial system, especially related to essential services.

C.   Outputs

The lending facility documents were executed in September 2020 and funds were disbursed in November 2020, thus ensuring the continuity of RPPL's operations. The company could sustain the amount of renewable electricity delivered to offtakers at the FY2020 baseline of 10,352 gigawatt hours per year. With its affiliates and subsidiaries, RPPL was able to meet 100% of its existing financial and performance-related obligations.

In addition, a gender action plan was integrated into RPPL's COVID-19 support measures. It included flexible and remote working arrangements with full pay, as well as information technology and communications support to at least 50% of all office workers. Other measures included support to employees for tackling issues related to domestic violence and mental health, which were exacerbated by the COVID-19 crisis. The CSR program of RPPL helped enhance entrepreneurship opportunities for women. By December 2021, at least eight women's self-help groups had started face mask production enterprises with training, mentoring, in-kind donations, and marketing support. As of 31 March 2021, at least 10,000 women and their families living near 15 or more project sites had received dry ration food packets, while at least ₹2.5 million worth of personal protective equipment and other medical equipment was donated to local hospitals and clinics.

D.   Outcomes

ADB's loan support ensured continuity in renewable power delivery to the domestic grid, which is an essential service business. It also helped RPPL continue salary payments to employees. The financing helped enhance gender equality through COVID-19-related staff arrangements as well as the CSR program that provided entrepreneurship opportunities for women.

Box 5.3 "Timely Help from ADB Helped Us Manage Cash Flow during the Pandemic"— ReNew Power

ReNew Power, which is engaged in selling power to the state distribution companies (DISCOMS), faced a liquidity crunch during the COVID-19 pandemic as there were delays in payments coming from these DISCOMS.

The lockdown and reduced economic activity also led to a temporary decline in power demand. Industries and commercial establishments are normally profitable DISCOM customers but they substantially reduced their power consumption during the lockdowns, which negatively impacted DISCOM cash flows.

"Our payment receivable cycles were stretched during the pandemic as DISCOMS across several states started delaying payments that led to liquidity pressure on the company," said Amit Rastogi, Vice President, Corporate Finance, ReNew Power Private Limited.

The liquidity crunch meant the company had to put on hold its capital expenditure plans while it catered to its committed payments to lenders.

"Timely help from ADB helped us manage these cash flows as we were able to timely serve our lenders as well as meet our working capital requirements," said Rastogi. "ADB is a long-term partner for us. It started as an equity partnership. And since then, we have grown a lot. We look forward to ADB providing structured finance, which is a first in the financing market. We would like to see more such products coming from ADB."

Source: Asian Development Bank.

Amit Rastogi, Vice President, Corporate Finance, ReNew Power Private Limited.

E. Impact

In the near term, the project helped reduce some of the adverse economic impacts of the pandemic by minimizing business disruptions in the energy sector. The ADB intervention was timely and in line with the Government of India's COVID-19 response priorities.

F. Looking Ahead

In the longer term, continued support to a private renewable power generator resulted in stable scaled-up operations and investment flexibility for the borrower, increased employment, and improved payment terms for the upstream and downstream agencies in the value chain. ADB's long-term working capital support to firms such as RPPL has been shown to have a positive and transformative impact on private sector operations as it is linked to targeted development outcomes in combination with a plan for improved environmental, health, and social safeguards.

6 ADB's Value Addition to India's COVID-19 Response

Enabling Support to India's COVID-19 Response

From the onset of the coronavirus disease (COVID-19) pandemic, ADB expedited approvals and disbursements for programs and projects. As the global economy slowed in the first few months of 2020, ADB fast-tracked its program and project processing to respond quickly to India's evolving development needs. Based on its presence in the country of more than 3 decades, ADB sought to understand India's specific needs and unique COVID-19 challenges to design relevant projects and programs.

ADB extended three TAs between 25 February 2020 and 22 April 2020. All three were related to disease management and urban health,[28] with an aggregate contract value of nearly $1.4 million. Immediately following these TAs, ADB responded with alacrity to the government's health system strengthening and economic package with support via the COVID-19 Active Response and Expenditure Support (CARES) Plus program. The pandemic presented ADB with the unprecedented challenge of working on a severely compressed timeline to quickly turn a loan request into disbursement without unduly compromising its rigorous internal processes. With regard to CARES, ADB cut through the concept clearance procedures and completed the fact-finding activity by 13 April 2020. Negotiations were completed on 15 April 2020, and by 28 April 2020, the board approved the two associated loans. Agreements were subsequently executed for a total assistance package of $1.5 billion.

Speedy clearances for projects and program followed throughout 2020–2021 in the areas of urban health care, a nationwide vaccination campaign, and the post-pandemic recovery effort. In India, as in other developing member countries (DMCs), ADB accelerated the clearance of sovereign requests and proposals by streamlining its internal processes and expediting consultations with agencies, project and assistance reviews, disbursements, and procurement.

Significantly, ADB also blended its COVID-19 response with ongoing, proposed, and future programs and projects to meet India's long-term development and sustainability goals. For instance, gender equity and social inclusion (GESI)-related outcomes were embedded into the monitoring framework for all supported activities. Sustainable health outcomes and urban developmental goals were also included in initiatives that were prioritized in response to the pandemic. A look at some of the ADB projects approved during 2020–2022 demonstrates the comprehensive support to India's short- and long-term development priorities and post-pandemic recovery effort (Table 6.1).

---

[28] Regional Support to Address the Outbreak of Novel Coronavirus (2019-nCoV) on 25 February 2020; Regional Support to Address the Outbreak of Coronavirus Disease 2019 and Potential Outbreaks of Other Communicable Diseases on 8 April 2020; and Strengthening Capacity of the National Urban Health Mission (Supplementary).

Table 6.1   Key ADB Commitments to the Government of India and the State Government Partners (2020-2022)

Commitment (amount in $ million)	Purpose	Partner
1,230	Strengthen electricity infrastructure in Assam, Maharashtra, Meghalaya, Tripura, and Uttar Pradesh.	State governments
850	Improve urban mobility through metro rail projects in Bengaluru, Karanataka and Chennai, Tamil Nadu.	State governments
570	Support sustainable urban development in secondary and smaller towns in Rajasthan and Madhya Pradesh.	State governments
500	Enhance urban mobility in the National Capital Region through Delhi–Meerut Regional Rapid Transit System.	Government of India
484	Strengthen road connectivity to facilitate industrial development in the Chennai–Kanyakumari Industrial Corridor (CKIC)[a] in Tamil Nadu.	State government
410	Upgrade major district roads and state highways in Assam; upgrade state highways in Rajasthan.	State governments
350	Accelerate policy actions to expand access to water, sanitation, and affordable housing in urban areas.	Government of India
300	Improve rural connectivity in Maharashtra.	State government
298	Improve urban services in Jharkhand, Tripura, and Uttarakhand.	State governments
251	Strengthen flood-risk management in Chennai, Tamil Nadu.	State governments
250	Support for raising India's industrial competitiveness and creating jobs.	Government of India
250	Promote wide-ranging reforms in the logistics sector of India to enhance efficiency.	Government of India
150	Provide affordable urban housing in Tamil Nadu.	State government
112	Set up Assam Skills University to expand industry-aligned capacity building and improve employability of the workforce.	State government
100	Promote agribusiness networks to increase farm incomes in Maharashtra.	State government
Nonsovereign (Private Sector) Operations[b]		
1,023	Projects included COVID-19 critical care, housing finance, food security, solar power, highways upgrade, energy efficiency, affordable housing for vulnerable groups, electric mobility, agribusiness, and crop nutrition.	
373	Supply Chain Finance Program and Microfinance Risk Participation and Guarantee Program promoted local currency lending to microfinance institutions across the Asia-Pacific region, including India.	

[a]   The CKIC is part of the ADB-supported East Coast Economic Corridor.

[b]   ADB commitments during 2020–2022.

Note: The list is not comprehensive and excludes some of the projects and programs already explained in this report.

Source: Asian Development Bank Member Fact Sheets, April 2022.

Gender Equity and Social Inclusion

Disasters and health emergencies often increase inequalities. The COVID-19 pandemic disproportionately affected the health, economic, social, and psychological well-being of women and children. Women in India not only faced an increased burden of household responsibilities during the lockdown, but also faced the adverse effects of the disease as frontline health workers,[29] limited access to health care facilities and financial resources for treatment, and the loss of livelihoods in the hard-hit and women-dominated informal sector. In response, the government programmed gender equity into almost all aspects of India's COVID-19 response (Figure 6.1).

Aligned to the government's objective, ADB embedded GESI outcomes into the monitoring framework for all supported activities. ADB estimated that 50% of the 200 million individuals that had cumulatively benefited from at least one program under Pradhan Mantri Garib Kalyan Yojana (PMGKY) were women. The monitoring framework targets contributed to additional gender equity-related operational priorities for 2030 as part of ADB's country partnership strategy in India.[30] These included:

(i)   enrollment of women in technical and vocational education and training and other job training programs,
(ii)   implementation or establishment of savings and insurance schemes for women, and
(iii) implementation of social assistance schemes (responsive to crisis) for women and girls.

Other programs such as the Subprogram 1 of the ADB-funded Sustainable Urban Development and Service Delivery Program promoted the mainstreaming of GESI measures while achieving universal coverage for water supply and sanitation. The operational guidelines issued by the Ministry of Housing and Urban Affairs, Government of India, to the states for program implementation included women's involvement in the following areas:

(i)   water demand management,
(ii)   operations and maintenance of water infrastructure,
(iii) capacity building (covering elected women representatives),
(iv)   tendering process,
(v)   water supply,
(vi)   used water management,
(vii) water bodies rejuvenation,
(viii) behavior change communication, and
(ix)   information, education, and communication.

Furthermore, during May–June 2022, GESI-sensitive and COVID-19-appropriate behavior messaging related to the spread of the omicron variant was conducted in 14 states, and a related outreach campaign promoted vaccinations for 15–17-year-olds among marginalized populations.

---

[29] Frontline health workers included accredited social health activists, doctors, and nurses.
[30] ADB. 2017. *Country Partnership Strategy: India, 2018–2022*. Manila.

Figure 6.1   Gender Equity and Social Inclusion during the COVID-19 Pandemic

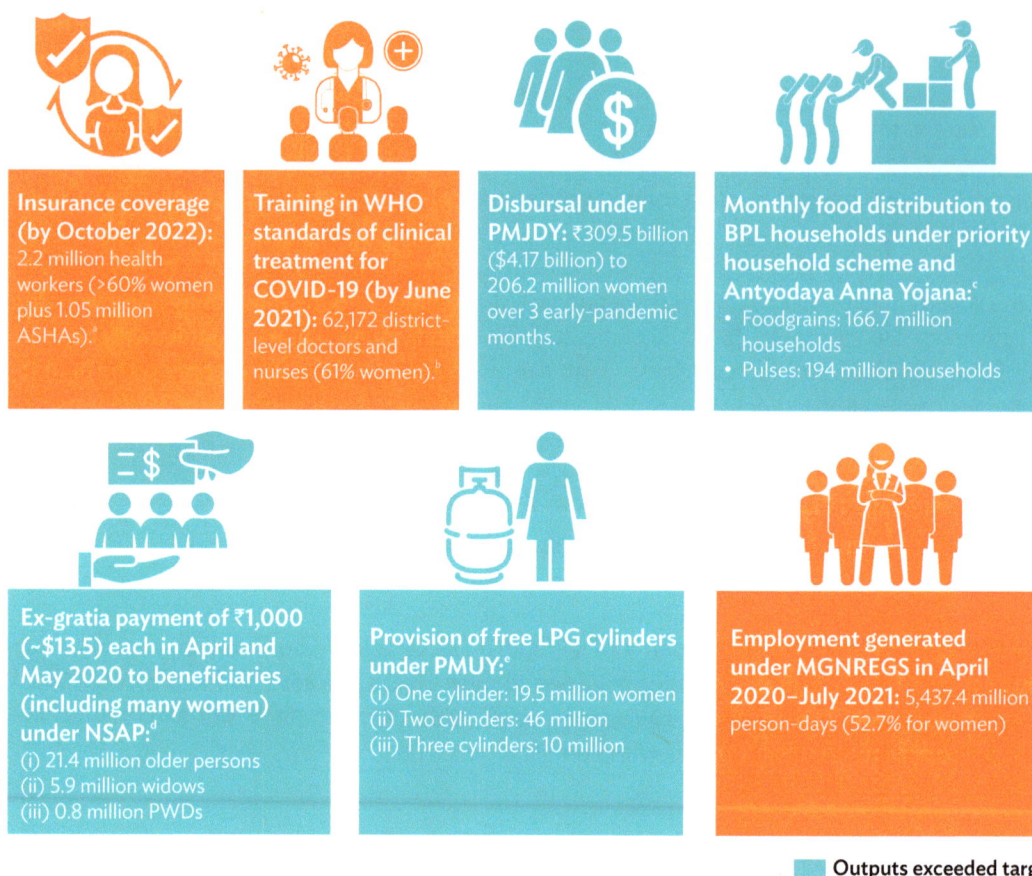

Insurance coverage (by October 2022): 2.2 million health workers (>60% women plus 1.05 million ASHAs).[a]

Training in WHO standards of clinical treatment for COVID-19 (by June 2021): 62,172 district-level doctors and nurses (61% women).[b]

Disbursal under PMJDY: ₹309.5 billion ($4.17 billion) to 206.2 million women over 3 early-pandemic months.

Monthly food distribution to BPL households under priority household scheme and Antyodaya Anna Yojana:[c]
- Foodgrains: 166.7 million households
- Pulses: 194 million households

Ex-gratia payment of ₹1,000 (~$13.5) each in April and May 2020 to beneficiaries (including many women) under NSAP:[d]
(i) 21.4 million older persons
(ii) 5.9 million widows
(iii) 0.8 million PWDs

Provision of free LPG cylinders under PMUY:[e]
(i) One cylinder: 19.5 million women
(ii) Two cylinders: 46 million
(iii) Three cylinders: 10 million

Employment generated under MGNREGS in April 2020–July 2021: 5,437.4 million person-days (52.7% for women)

■ **Outputs exceeded targets**

ASHA = accredited social health activist, BPL = below poverty line, MGNREGS = Mahatma Gandhi National Rural Employment Guarantee Scheme, NSAP = National Social Assistance Programme, PMJDY = Pradhan Mantri Jan Dhan Yojana, PMUY = Pradhan Mantri Ujjwala Yojana, PWD = person with disabilities, WHO = World Health Organization.

[a] Government of India, Ministry of Health and Family Welfare. 2022. "Pradhan Mantri Garib Kalyan Package: Insurance Scheme for Health Workers fighting COVID-19" extended for a further period of 180 days. Press release through Press Information Bureau. 19 April. https://pib.gov.in/PressReleaseIframePage.aspx?PRID=1817977.

[b] Government of India, Ministry of Health and Family Welfare. 2021. *ADB CARES Progress Report up to June 2021.* New Delhi.

[c] Support provided in the initial pandemic period was extended over a period. This brought relief to women in the beneficiary families.

[d] Government of India, Ministry of Rural Development, National Social Assistance Programme. 2020. Letter No. L-11014/01/2017. 23 November.

[e] Data received from the Ministry of Petroleum and Natural Gas, Government of India, on 8 March 2021.

Capacity Building

ADB's capacity building support aligned to its lending programs during the pandemic was central to the success of these programs. Under the COVID-19 Pandemic Response Option, the Government of India aimed to build a resilient workforce in the clinical management of public health emergencies. All doctors and nurses in district hospitals were trained in accordance with the World Health Organization standards of clinical treatment and management of COVID-19.[31] ADB's direct and indirect support strengthened governance, institutional capacity, and individual skills to manage the health emergency. Specifically, the CARES TA supported the

(i)   development of the Government of India's Emergency COVID-19 Response Plan Phase 1 and Phase 2 for state-level contingency planning and guidance documents on enabling the delivery of essential services and reproductive and child health services both during and after the pandemic,

(ii)   analysis of emerging infectious disease contingency plans for the management of the pandemic in states and Union Territories, and

(iii) building of a sustainable and resilient health care delivery system at the national and state levels to respond to future outbreaks of infectious diseases.

During periodic reporting under components of the CARES Plus program,[32] ADB provided monitoring and evaluation support on disease surveillance; data analytics and insights; and improved information technology-enabled reporting, including for critical health supplies such as medical oxygen (Box 6.1).

Box 6.1   Innovation to Monitor Medical Oxygen Demand–Supply

Demand for medical oxygen increased dramatically during the pandemic. Efficiency in tracking the availability of and demand for medical oxygen was of immense value in dealing with disease management. The CARES TA supported the development of three digital innovations:

(i)   a MedSupply Portal to track the progress of implementation on a real-time basis,

(ii)   an OxyCare Portal (in collaboration with the National Informatics Centre) to create a repository for all data related to oxygen infrastructure and ensure adoption at the state level, and

(iii) an Oxygen Demand Aggregation System Portal (developed by National Health Authority) to aggregate oxygen demand at the health facility level and infer nationwide real-time oxygen demand.

Source: Asian Development Bank.

In addition, regular in-depth interactions between the CARES program management unit, ADB, and the Ministry of Health and Family Welfare, Government of India, led to the development of digital modules for capacity and skill building among health care staff active on the frontline of COVID-19 management (Box 6.2).[33]

---

[31]   Government of India, Ministry of Health and Family Welfare. 2021. *ADB CARES: Progress Report up to June 2021*. New Delhi.

[32]   Updates were reported on (i) macroeconomic conditions, (ii) budget and expenditure statements, (iii) implementation progress on the pandemic response and health system strengthening, (iv) the Integrated Health Information Portal, and (v) ongoing capacity-building efforts.

[33]   Government of India, Department of Personnel and Training. Integrated-Government Online Training Portal. https://diksha.gov.in/igot/.

Box 6.2   The Integrated Government Online Training Platform

To meet the training needs of personnel (including civil servants) involved in pandemic relief operations, the Government of India operationalized e-learning modules on the Integrated Government Online Training system. ADB supported the development of 50 e-learning modules in multiple Indian languages to target doctors, nurses, students, police, technicians, and other frontline workers. The modules included training content on the basics of COVID-19, clinical management, intensive care unit care management, infection prevention and care, proper use of personal protective equipment, quarantine and isolation, sample collection and testing, psychological care of patients, and pregnancy and pediatric care. Other e-learning modules were developed to inform and train key agencies and citizens—including police and social security agencies, resident welfare associations, recovered patients, and youth volunteers—in managing future contagions.

Through 31 December 2020, about 2.5 million people had registered for courses on the platform and about 1.9 million people had completed them.

Source: Asian Development Bank.

Through the CARES TA, ADB supported activities and studies to enhance the capacity of institutions and government officials tasked with executing sub-schemes under the PMGKY. These included the monitoring of social protection measures through essential commodity price monitoring and analysis, and tracking the impact of health systems upgrade initiatives. The TA also supported disease surveillance enhancement to improve overall public health, including the pilot rollout of the Integrated Health Information Portal, a next-generation robust disease surveillance system. All eight government agencies[34] implementing the various health and social security sub-schemes undertook capacity enhancement and service delivery improvement measures that were supported by ADB.

The CARES TA also contributed to the development of a seamlessly integrated and robust system to collect, store, report, monitor, and analyze price data for essential commodities from multiple sources through data quality and validation checks that provide actionable insights.

Structural Reforms

The Government of India undertook several reform measures to put the country firmly on the path to recovery. Structural reforms were targeted to boost investment in public health, facilitate the ease of doing business, enhance employment opportunities, and promote infrastructure investment. Key reforms included (i) boosting investments in public health, including ramping up the establishment of health and wellness centers in rural and urban areas to prepare India for future pandemics; (ii) revising the definition of a micro, small, or medium-sized enterprise for raising investment limits to enable firms to achieve economies of scale in production, and avoid splitting of enterprises to remain "small" to continue availing official assistance; (iii) introducing the One Nation One Ration Card initiative for the nationwide portability of rations cards; (iv) amending government procurement rules; and (v) implementing policy reforms to enhance competitiveness and domestic manufacturing, with accompanying social welfare schemes and infrastructure investments.

---

[34]   (i) Ministry of Consumer Affairs, Food and Public Distribution; (ii) Ministry of Agriculture and Farmers Welfare; (iii) Ministry of Rural Development; (iv) Ministry of Petroleum and Natural Gas; (v) Ministry of Labour and Employment; (vi) MOHFW; (vii) Department of Financial Services; and (viii) Department of Expenditure.

ADB provided support to some of these reform efforts including strengthening governance structures for pandemic care, enhancing the preparedness of the health care sector for future pandemics, promoting industrial corridor development to boost manufacturing, and strengthening urban service delivery. The CARES Plus program sought to strengthen the reform process by ensuring the continuity of benefits would extend beyond the life of the program.[35] This entailed the following:

(i)   strengthening public health infrastructure for pandemic preparedness,
(ii)   developing central institutions as mentor institutions,
(iii)   improving the surveillance of infectious diseases and outbreak response,
(iv)   reinforcing surveillance at ports of entry into the country, and
(v)   strengthening disaster and epidemic preparedness and bio-security preparedness and research.

As part of its COVID-19 economic recovery focus, the government aims to significantly accelerate reforms in urban service delivery. ADB, through its Sustainable Urban Development and Service Delivery Program, is supporting the implementation of policy actions that are crucial for structural urban reforms linked to (i) improving water supply and sanitation service delivery outcomes, (ii) enhancing access to affordable housing, and (iii) implementing the XV Finance Commission's recommendation for performance-based fiscal transfers to states and urban local bodies.

Other Contributions

ADB support to various government initiatives for pandemic response and recovery is helping India achieve its Sustainable Development Goals (SDGs) milestones. For example, the CARES Plus program directly contributed to the SDGs on ending poverty and hunger, reducing inequalities and increasing gender equity, promoting good health and well-being, and building stronger partnerships.[36] Other projects contributed to SDGs on clean water and sanitation; sustainable cities and communities; industry, innovation and infrastructure; and decent work and economic growth.

---

[35]   Compiled from the Project Completion Report (Program Number: 54182-001. Loan Numbers: 3915 and 3916.). *India: COVID-19 Active Response and Expenditure Support Program.* November 2022.
[36]   Footnote 35.

7   ADB Partnering with India on the Economic Recovery Path

To limit the pandemic's lingering impact on India's economic growth trajectory, the Government of India is pursuing initiatives and enabling policies that will reinvigorate the economy. As part of the Atmanirbhar Bharat Abhiyaan (Self-Reliant India Campaign) package, the government and the central bank have announced several initiatives to help small businesses and boost productivity. The pillars of the campaign are (i) boosting the economy, (ii) creating modern infrastructure, (iii) promoting technology-driven systems, (iv) benefiting from vibrant demographics, and (v) fully utilizing the power of demand and supply. This package was backed by government reforms across seven sectors that aim to put the economy on the recovery path. A comprehensive post-pandemic recovery action plan was prepared that sought to improve access to infrastructure and services, revamp the health and education sectors, invest in skilling and vocational training for a post-pandemic world, develop economic corridors to generate more manufacturing jobs, and promote smart cities.

Aligning to the government's priorities, ADB combined its pandemic response with strong support for the country's post-pandemic recovery path beyond the peak health emergency years of 2020–2021. Some of the key programs and projects ADB approved during this period that provided non-health pandemic support included the Industrial Corridor Development Program, Assam Skill University Project, Sustainable Urban Development and Service Delivery Program, and Maharashtra Rural Connectivity Improvement Project to buttress a range of government initiatives. These projects will support efforts for policy and regulatory reforms in key sectors of the economy, build better infrastructure and services, and promote skill development that will benefit people directly.

Industrial Corridor Development Program

The impact of the COVID-19 pandemic was severely felt by India's manufacturing sector, whose share of the country's GDP had already been stagnant at 13%–16% of GDP before March 2020.[37] Growth in manufacturing exports has been traditionally weak, resulting in limited participation in global value chains (GVCs). Manufacturing has also failed to absorb the country's growing labor force. It employs only 12% of the labor force, which is less than half the share employed by the services sector. Further, India's low competitiveness in manufacturing is reflected in the declining contribution of manufacturing to GDP, India's low share of world manufacturing exports (less than 2.5%),[38] and a low number of workers in the sector.

The pandemic spread further strained the manufacturing sector due to the abrupt drop in demand, broken supply chains, a liquidity crunch, and a loss of productivity due to lockdown measures. The government has introduced various policy initiatives to increase the share of manufacturing in GDP and raise productivity and competitiveness.

---

[37]   Government of India, Ministry of Finance. Various years. *Economic Survey of India.* New Delhi.
[38]   Government of India, Ministry of Finance. 2023. *Economic Survey of India 2022–23.* New Delhi.

During COVID-19, the government announced additional reforms under the Atmanirbhar Bharat Abhiyan (Self-Reliant India Campaign) in May 2020, focusing on the rejuvenation of domestic manufacturing and greater integration with GVCs, including the promotion of foreign direct investment in 13 priority manufacturing sectors.

The government's Make in India program recognizes industrial corridors as a development tool to raise India's manufacturing competitiveness and enable it to integrate better with GVCs, particularly in Southeast Asia and East Asia. This is being pursued through the multipronged National Industrial Corridor Development Program (NICDP), an ambitious program that aims to develop both brownfield and greenfield industrial clusters within corridors.

The overall aim is to increase the competitiveness of the manufacturing sector, strengthen national supply chains and links with regional and GVCs, and create jobs.

India's industrial corridor development program started with the Delhi–Mumbai Industrial Corridor in 2007 and expanded to five corridors in 2017. The program has been further expanded to develop 11 corridors covering 17 states with 32 projects in 4 phases. National Industrial Corridor Development and Implementation Trust (NICDIT) and National Industrial Corridor Development Corporation (NICDC) have been set up to provide an apex institutional framework under the guidance of the Department for Promotion of Industry and Internal Trade.

Overview

India's push to expand its industrial corridor development as part of the strategy to boost its manufacturing sector needed to overcome several existing constraints including greater center–state coordination to oversee the activities of the NICDP. This required streamlining institutional framework for such coordination and integrated project development in the corridor areas.

As a development partner, ADB was suitably positioned to support the government's corridor development strategy, building on its previous experience as the lead partner in the development of East Coast Economic Corridor (ECEC) since 2014. ADB's support to ECEC included establishing institutional frameworks for corridor development, developing single-window clearance platforms to integrate all investor applications at one place, promoting reforms for facilitating businesses, establishing housing for industrial workers, and developing framework for resilient and sustainable infrastructure.

Lessons learnt from this experience paved the way in October 2021 for the ADB-approved Subprogram 1, valued at $250 million, to support the NICDP.

ADB supported the development of the Visakhapatnam-Chennai Industrial Corridor that is part of the East Coast Economic Corridor.

Objective

The overarching objective of the program is to boost India's manufacturing competitiveness and to increase the share of manufacturing in GDP. The ADB-supported program was designed to strengthen the enabling environment through institutional and regulatory reforms for effective implementation of the NICDP, building on ADB's state-level strategic studies and investment programs for the development of industrial corridors. This will lead to better and more efficient planning for industrial nodes and will facilitate private investment.

Outputs

Prior policy actions under subprogram 1 were completed across the following reform areas from April 2020 to January 2022:

(i) Reforms under Subprogram 1 aimed to improve the institutional environment around industrial corridor development and introduce gender-inclusive strategies for fulfilling industrial skills needs. Both policy actions included under this reform area were achieved. The institutional mandate of the NICDC was expanded to cover six new corridors in addition to five existing ones. The NICDC and the National Skills Development Corporation jointly prepared skills development programs to upgrade skills of local labor force and to address skill gaps with a gender focus.

(ii) Sustainable and green infrastructure planning was incorporated at the node level, and challenges related to economic and spatial planning were addressed at the city and regional levels. Access to long-term finance was improved for private sector firms.

(iii) Reforms to enhance transparency, streamline business processes, and increase investor outreach activities were supported to draw private and foreign investment to clusters and industrial corridors.

Outcomes

The program is designed to improve investment climate for industrial corridor development. It will be measured through increased investment flow in corridor areas, both from the public and private sectors.

Impact

The program will lay the foundation for future support to states by strengthening the relevant institutional and regulatory frameworks, aligning national and state policies for planning, and facilitating the integrated development of industrial corridors.

Looking Ahead

Soon after the completion of Subprogram 1, policy actions for Subprogram 2 were laid out for implementation during February 2022–December 2024. ADB will provide a TA to roll out a complement of services to enhance knowledge, policy, and operations frameworks.

The ADB intervention also put in place a Post-Program Partnership Framework to support the NICDIT in (i) developing a long-term finance strategy, (ii) preparing it to obtain regulatory approvals from the Securities and Exchange Board of India for debt finance, and (iii) using debentures and bonds for debt financing. The trust will also support low-income states, including India's northeastern states, in strengthening their industrial policies and regulatory regimes for corridor development and in identifying and participating in regional value chains across South Asia and Southeast Asia.

Investment in Skilling and Vocational Training in Assam

Unemployment and underemployment have been long-standing challenges to India's development. The hinterlands of northern and central India and northeastern India are marked by poor access to education and economic opportunities. The traditional cultural and behavioral influences in these parts of the country have compounded their challenges. The unskilled and semi-skilled remain dependent upon traditional sources of income with low value-added—such as farming, construction, and industrial labor. This results in significant labor migration to large urban agglomerations.

A model of the upcoming Assam Skill University that is being developed as part of an ADB-funded project.

Workers lacking modern skills from these regions faced significant job losses during the COVID-19 pandemic, particularly the youth. The breakdown of previously functioning business models and loss of livelihoods accentuated the need for re-skilling and upskilling among the youth. Specifically, the disruptive health emergency underscored the need for Indian youth to develop modern skills. Such development can help those from regions such as the northeastern India to seek productive employment, move toward better paying jobs, and aspire to be more enterprising—thereby closing the gap with other parts of India.

The Government of Assam aims to develop a university that will build a skills education and training ecosystem as a logical antecedent to decent employment for the youth of Assam and the rest of northeastern India. ADB approved a $112 million loan to assist the state government to set up the Assam Skill University (ASU), aligned to the objectives of India's National Skill Development Mission (Box 7.1).

> **Box 7.1   Skill India Mission to Boost the Employability of Youth**
>
> The Government of India launched Skill India Mission in 2015 to empower the youth of the country with skill sets that make them more employable and productive in their work environment. Skill India offers courses across 40 sectors in the country which are aligned to the standards recognized by both the industry and the government under the National Skill Qualification Framework.[a] The courses help a person focus on practical delivery of work and help enhance technical expertise so that they are ready from day one and companies don't have to invest into customized training to suit the job profile.
>
> Over 20 central government ministries and departments are currently implementing skill development initiatives to enhance skill levels of millions of people, including school children, on a pan-India basis to create skilled workforce as per the needs of the industry.
>
> The National Education Policy 2020 provides impetus to the mission through integration and mainstreaming of vocational education with general education, helping students acquire skills to meet the needs of the industries and to improve the quality of education.
>
> [a]   Government of India, Ministry of Skill Development and Entrepreneurship. https://www.msde.gov.in/en/about-msde/background.
> Source: Asian Development Bank.

Overview

Both economically and demographically, Assam is the largest state in northeastern India (Appendix 2). It occupies a strategic position for various regional cooperation programs.[39] The state remains largely rural with underdeveloped infrastructure, and its economy is dominated by natural resource-based products that are characterized by low value-add. Natural hazard events such as cyclones and floods occur here frequently. In Assam, not only is poverty higher than the national average, its educational attainment—technical and vocational education and training (TVET) and higher education—and labor force participation rates are also lower. The limited availability of a skilled workforce in Assam also adds to these constraints. These indicators were most likely further adversely affected by the COVID-19 pandemic.

ADB studies related to northeastern India have recommended corridor-based industrial growth with linkages to global supply chains as a strategy for Assam's economic development. A necessary component of such development is a high-quality workforce with employable skills.[40] Assam's socioeconomic development will, therefore, hinge upon the availability of skilled human resources, TVET, and higher education. Thus, the Government of Assam initiated the ASU by promulgating the Assam Skill University Act, 2020.

Objective

The ADB-supported project aims to create pathways for skills progression with seamless mobility between secondary education, TVET, and higher education. Complementing the loan is a TA grant of $1.15 million to provide expertise in the design and management of environmentally sustainable and climate-resilient buildings and facilities. The TA will also assist in the development of digital platforms and tools for teaching, learning, and career management, especially in the post-pandemic context.

---

[39]   These programs include Bangladesh–Bhutan–India–Nepal (BBIN) and Bay of Bengal Initiative for Multisectoral Technical and Economic Cooperation (BIMSTEC).

[40]   ADB. 2021. *Assam as India's Gateway to ASEAN.* Manila. | ADB. 2021. *North East Economic Corridor: Bringing People and Markets Together.* Presentation prepared for the virtual workshops on North East Economic Corridor study organized in collaboration with the Government of India's Department of Promotion of Industry and Internal Trade. 20 April; 18, 25 and 30 June; and 5 July 2021.

Overall, the ASU project aims to contribute to SDGs such as decent employment for all and inclusive and sustainable infrastructure and industrial development in Assam.

Output

In addition to the design and construction of the ASU campus and facilities, the project will support the development of sustainable management and operating systems for the university, viable business models, and faculty development programs. Industry-aligned and flexible skills education and training programs will be designed and delivered using various modalities such as online, on- and off-campus, and hub-and-spoke approaches.

Unlike conventional universities, the ASU will enroll a wider range of Indian society, including dropouts and graduates from secondary education, TVET, and higher education, as well as professionals and members of the working-age population. It will support opportunities and business processes that have been accelerated by the COVID-19 pandemic by equipping its students with appropriate skills. The ASU will also support local entrepreneurs and businesses through entrepreneurship education and support, applied research and development, and technology transfers.

Outcomes

The ASU will energize the state's economy by supporting local entrepreneurs and businesses in two ways: (i) supplying skilled personnel for their business activities; and (ii) providing entrepreneurship education and support, applied research and development, and technology transfers (Box 7.2).

Box 7.2   Government of Assam's Vision for the Assam Skill University

The Assam Skill University seeks to:

- distinguish itself as a premium institution with its campus equipped with state-of-the-art facilities and technologies;
- conduct skills education and training integrated with higher education, applied research and development, entrepreneurship education, and support;
- raise skill levels to enhance the productivity and competitiveness of industries in Assam and northeast India; and
- cater to the needs of its students, domestic technical and vocational training centers, and higher education institutions and industries in India as well as in neighboring countries.

Source: Asian Development Bank.

Impact

Through support for the ASU, ADB aims to contribute to decent employment for all—in line with SDG 8—and to promote inclusive and sustainable infrastructure and industrial development in Assam and other states in northeastern India, while participating in the ongoing digital and green transformations that were accelerated by the onset of the COVID-19 pandemic.

Looking Ahead

The ASU is expected to start operations in 2024 at its interim campus in Guwahati. The main campus at Mangaldai will be ready by 2025.

Sustainable Urban Development and Service Delivery Program

While health care was the service in highest demand during the COVID-19 pandemic, cities in India also faced challenges in providing other basic services, especially for the urban poor. The pandemic accentuated the need to enhance hygienic practices and expand access to clean water and sanitation facilities in urban areas. It also highlighted an urgent need to provide affordable housing for migrant laborers and poor populations, and to safeguard their livelihoods. Further, the provision of high-quality urban infrastructure aligns with government programs that promote cities as engines of growth.

India's urban areas are projected to have 876 million dwellers by 2050,[41] up from 460 million in 2020.[42] While this will present many challenges, rapid urbanization can also generate economic opportunities, create jobs, and improve competitiveness, thus driving stronger growth. Simultaneously, it presents other challenges as rural poor migrate to the cities in search of better livelihood leading to urban sprawls with increase in unplanned development and informal settlements. To support the government's long-term urban sector development plans, which were further validated by the growing demand for urban services throughout the pandemic, ADB approved Subprogram 1 of the Sustainable Urban Development and Service Delivery Program, with a value of $350 million, in December 2021.

Overview

Urban development in India has not been able to maximize the economic benefits associated with increasing urbanization. With uncontrolled urbanization, many cities are not equipped to provide basic urban services such as water supply, sanitation, and housing to their increasing urban populations. Poorly managed urbanization has curbed social gains, and compromised environmental sustainability, exposing many people to worsening climate and disaster risks. Several factors have constrained India's development of its urban sector to date: insufficient urban service delivery, including inadequate private sector participation; funding limitations and underdeveloped financial capacities of urban local bodies (ULBs), which results in overdependence on fiscal transfers; and insufficient promotion of an urban reform agenda.

The Government of India, as part of its COVID-19 economic recovery reform initiative, significantly accelerated reforms in urban service delivery. On 1 October 2021, the government launched the Atal Mission for Rejuvenation and Urban Transformation 2.0 (AMRUT 2.0),[43] a national flagship urban water mission, which aims to achieve universal coverage of piped water supply across all urban areas, and improved sanitation in 500 large towns. The government also established a new urban rental housing program for migrant laborers and poor people to safeguard their livelihoods as COVID-19 recovery program. Further, in line with the report of India's XV Finance Commission, routine fiscal devolution is made conditional on local revenue improvements.

---

[41] United Nations, Department of Economic and Social Affairs, Population Division. 2019. *World Urbanization Prospects: The 2018 Revision*. New York. https://population.un.org/wup/Publications/Files/WUP2018-Report.pdf.

[42] Government of India, Ministry of Housing and Urban Affairs. 2019. *Consultation Paper on City GDP Measurement Framework*. New Delhi. https://smartnet.niua.org/sites/default/files/resources/city_gdp_measurement_framework.pdf.

[43] AMRUT was launched in 2015 to improve urban services (water supply, sewerage and septage management, stormwater drainage, nonmotorized urban transport, and green space) in 500 selected towns with a population of more than 0.1 million (Census of India 2011) and some other towns. To date, about 5,891 projects worth $11.1 billion are either completed or under implementation, and the mission has provided 11.2 million water connections and 8.7 million sewer connections to households and sewage treatment plants with a total capacity of 1,800 million liters per day. As part of municipal reforms, 468 ULBs were credit rated and nine ULBs raised municipal bonds under AMRUT. In addition, 439 ULBs have established online building permit systems as part of improved e-governance. | Government of India, Ministry of Housing and Urban Affairs. https://mohua.gov.in/.

ADB-supported Atal Mission for Rejuvenation and Urban Transformation 2.0 aims to achieve universal coverage of piped water supply across all urban areas.

Objective

The ADB-funded program addresses the government's priority for enhancing delivery of basic urban services as part of its COVID-19 recovery focus. This is ADB's first national policy-based loan that aims to rejuvenate India's urban sector through enabling reforms and policies targeted to improve access to basic services and affordable housing to urban migrants, industrial workers, and poor people, all of whom were especially impacted by the pandemic. ADB's assistance for the program was envisaged as two subprograms of $350 million each. Subprogram 1 established essential policies and guidelines at the national level, while subprogram 2 will target the specific reform actions and program proposals at state and ULB levels, which will be enforced through performance-based grants.

Subprogram 1 also included an additional TA grant of $1.5 million to provide knowledge and advisory support to Ministry of Housing and Urban Affairs and state governments toward rolling out policy reforms under AMRUT 2.0 in state and ULBs, mainly under subprogram 2.

Outputs

Subprogram 1 established essential national policies and guidelines that aimed to improve basic urban services under three major reform areas: (i) AMRUT 2.0 mission, approved by the National Cabinet with a financial outlay of over $37 billion, aims to ensure universal access to water supply and improved sanitation services, preferentially benefiting the urban poor population and women; (ii) a program was approved under Pradhan Mantri Awas Yojana (Housing for All) - Urban (PMAY-U) for providing affordable rental housing complexes for improved access to rental housing for urban migrant and industrial workers, working women, and poor persons; and (iii) the recommendations of the XV Finance Commission implemented making central fiscal transfers to ULBS conditional to performance on local revenue improvements. These reforms would help improve ULBs' local financial resource generation and promote urban governance improvement.

Outcomes

The reforms of AMRUT 2.0 and the XV Finance Commission are geared towards water security by reducing nonrevenue water, meeting 20% of water demand through recycled water, water body rejuvenation, groundwater management, and ensuring financial sustainability through annual revision of user charges, property tax reforms, ULB credit worthiness enhancement, and urban planning reforms. The reforms serve to increase the climate resilience of the urban water sector.

Impact

The program aims to transform cities into economically vibrant and environmentally sustainable habitats that provide equitable access to basic infrastructure, public services, and opportunities for all inhabitants.

Looking Ahead

ADB will play an important role in implementing reforms in states and ULBs through continuous engagement in coordination with other development partners. The focus will be on lower-income states, which require support in capacity building, institution strengthening, and policy reforms. ADB will continue to support the government's renewed urban strategy for sustainable urban growth through land use planning, transit-oriented development, and urban agglomeration. ADB was a knowledge partner to the Infrastructure Working Group under India's G20 presidency (2023), which had a theme of Financing Cities of Tomorrow (Inclusive, Resilient and Sustainable). ADB prepared a deliverable on Capacity Building of Urban Administrations for Cities of Tomorrow. As a follow-on engagement, ADB is engaging with various cities to support them to enhance their own-source revenues and creditworthiness, improve access to private sector financing including municipal bonds, and generate a bankable pipeline of projects.

Maharashtra Rural Connectivity Improvement Project

A 2006 ADB analysis based on in-depth case studies concluded that poor and very poor populations benefit substantially from rural roads through improved access to state-provided health, education, agricultural extension, and information services. Such improvements reduce the perception of isolation and remoteness among poor and very poor people, which was especially felt during the COVID-19 pandemic.[44]

Rural roads comprise 71.4% of India's road network of 6.3 million kilometers (km), the second largest in the world,[45] which caters to a rural population of 909 million (65% of the total population).[46] A large part of the 2.7 million km rural road network is in poor condition. Given India's large rural population and the limitations of infrastructure and services in these areas, rural India significantly exceeded urban India in terms of the number of COVID-19 infections, with rural areas also reporting a disproportionately larger number of deaths. Maharashtra was the Indian state most impacted by COVID-19 through the end of June 2021, with more than 6 million COVID-19 cases, or about 20% of the India's total, and 30.7% of all deaths due to the disease in

---

44   Hemalata Hettige. 2006. *When Do Rural Roads Benefit the Poor and How: An In-Depth Analysis Based on Case Studies.* Asian Development Bank. Manila. https://www.adb.org/sites/default/files/publication/29406/when-rural-roads-benefit-poor.pdf.

45   Government of India, Ministry of Road Transport and Highways. 2022. *Basic Road Statistics in India 2018–19.* New Delhi. https://morth.nic.in/sites/default/files/Basic%20Road%20Statistics%20in%20India-2018-19.pdf.

46   World Bank staff estimates based on the United Nations Population Division's World Urbanization Prospects: 2018 Revision. https://data.worldbank.org/indicator/SP.RUR.TOTL?locations=IN.

India.[47] Improved road connectivity might have saved more lives in Maharashtra by allowing for the delivery of better critical health care services in rural areas. Further, physical connectivity is crucial for the quality of life and economic opportunities of Maharashtra's rural population. To help improve rural connectivity and accelerate the state's post-pandemic recovery, ADB approved $300 million of additional financing in July 2021 to the ongoing Maharashtra Rural Connectivity Improvement Project (MRCIP).

Overview

Maharashtra accounts for the largest network of rural roads in the country at 420,000 km (of which 74.1% are surfaced).[48] However, in terms of density of rural roads, Maharashtra's 6.7 km per 1,000 rural population and 1,428 km per 1,000 km^2 of rural area lags well behind Assam's 12.6 km per 1,000 rural population and 4,749 km^2 per 1,000 km^2 of rural area.[49, 50] ADB supports the expansion of rural connectivity in the state through the ongoing MRCIP (approved in August 2019), which aims to upgrade 2,100 km of rural roads in 34 districts to all-weather standards.

ADB-supported expansion of rural connectivity in the state of Maharashtra through the Maharashtra Rural Connectivity Improvement Project.

---

[47] https://www.orfonline.org/research/winning-the-covid-19-battle-in-rural-india-a-blueprint-for-action/.

[48] Footnote 45.

[49] Data on rural road length drawn from Government of India, Ministry of Road Transport and Highways. 2022. Footnote 45. | Data on state wise rural population as on 1 April 2018 drawn from https://ejalshakti.gov.in/IMISReports/Reports/BasicInformation/rpt_RWS_RuralPopulation_S.aspx?Rep=0.

[50] Area of rural Maharashtra at 0.3 million square kilometer as reported in the Census of India 2011. https://censusindia.gov.in/nada/index.php/catalog/42526/download/46152/A-1_NO_OF_VILLAGES_TOWNS_HOUSEHOLDS_POPULATION_AND_AREA.xlsx. | Data on state wise rural population as on 1 April 2018 drawn from https://ejalshakti.gov.in/IMISReports/Reports/BasicInformation/rpt_RWS_RuralPopulation_S.aspx?Rep=0. | Rural road length per 1,000 square km of rural Assam as reported in Government of India, Ministry of Road Transport and Highways. 2022. Footnote 45.

Objective

The additional financing for MRCIP will scale up the ongoing project to improve connectivity between habitations, productive agricultural lands, and economic growth centers across Maharashtra. These development activities and their outcomes will enhance employment opportunities for the rural population, which has been severely impacted by COVID-19 and associated lockdowns.

Outputs

The additional financing will help improve the safety conditions of 1,100 rural roads and 230 bridges spanning a total of 2,900 km. The roads will be made climate-resilient and have safety features to withstand extreme weather events such as floods. For this, new technologies such as asphalt blended with plastic waste and pre-cast concrete arch bridges will be used.

Outcomes

The MRCIP offered much-needed local employment opportunities in rural areas during a period of economic hardship caused by the pandemic and provided a safety net to reduce financial distress precipitated by the large-scale reverse migration to rural areas.[51] Apart from this immediate outcome, ADB support also contributed to sustained long-term benefits such as the improved conditions and safety of selected rural roads, including upgraded maintenance and climate resilience,[52] resulting in better rural connectivity. The capacities of rural infrastructure agencies were enhanced and safe-driving awareness raised among road users. Finally, road transport efficiency in 34 districts in Maharashtra will be increased further from 2025 to 2027, with the average travel time along project roads declining by 50% (2018 baseline: 4 minutes/km) and the average daily vehicle-km measure increasing to 1,269,800 (2018 baseline: 837,750 vehicle-km).

Impact

The MRCIP is accelerating Maharashtra's COVID-19 economic recovery by generating rural employment, improving agricultural productivity and food security, strengthening agricultural value chains, and furthering agriculture marketing reforms. It is expected that the project will generate about 3.1 million person-days of employment for local communities, of which at least 25% will be for women, during the infrastructure construction and maintenance periods. The project will enhance farmers' access to markets and service centers, which will contribute to improved agricultural productivity and increased farmer incomes. All-weather roads and the construction of needed bridges will also promote investment in agribusiness and enhance agriculture value chains. ADB's overall support for improved rural connectivity will help increase the average growth rate of agriculture and allied activities to more than 5% per year by 2030, in line the state's strategic development plan, *Vision 2030*.[53]

ADB Support to India in the Post-Pandemic Phase

The COVID-19 pandemic started waning in India by the second quarter of 2022. Beyond the tumultuous pandemic period, ADB assistance in 2022 was focused on supporting India's fast recovery. Aligned to the government's endeavor, a critical objective of ADB's operations was to reinvigorate economic activity to generate formal jobs, improve productivity, and create livelihood opportunities held back by the pandemic.

51   Amrit Ajay Sharma and Swapna Bist Joshi. 2020. Rural Roads are Key to Helping Society's Most Vulnerable. *Asian Development Blog.* 17 September. https://blogs.adb.org/blog/rural-roads-are-key-helping-societys-most-vulnerable.
52   Roads were selected from a priority list in the district road development plans. Safety measures include cautionary and information signs, guard posts, and speed breakers.
53   State Government of Maharashtra, Planning Department. 2018. *Vision 2030.* Mumbai. https://plan.maharashtra.gov.in/Sitemap/plan/pdf/final_Vision_Eng_Oct2017.pdf.

To achieve this, ADB adopted an integrated and multisectoral approach and prioritized transformational projects that would ensure sustained, long-term benefits to communities. The project design ensured inclusivity of all beneficiaries by especially catering to the needs of women, children, lower-skilled workers, vulnerable communities, and also aspirational states.

Tied to these objectives, ADB approved several projects in 2022 that targeted improving India's logistics efficiency to spur infrastructure development, enhancing connectivity of urban and rural communities, upgrading urban services across states, promoting industrial development, and improving energy security.

One significant intervention was a $250 million loan to support government reforms in India's logistics sector, a key area of government's focus to enhance efficiency of the country's logistics ecosystem as part of the government's goal of strengthening infrastructure under Pradhan Mantri Gati Shakti initiative. Improving its logistics efficiency is tied to India's endeavor to raise competitiveness of its products in the domestic and global markets. ADB support is helping the government develop an institutional and policy framework for incentivizing private sector participation in multimodal logistics projects. Earlier, ADB had provided TA to drive policy and institutional reforms by supporting the development of the draft National Logistics Policy launched by Prime Minister Narendra Modi in September 2022.

Another key intervention during the year was ADB assistance to expand the metro network in Chennai aimed to enhance urban mobility, reduce congestion, and improve livability in the Chennai Metropolitan Area. ADB pursued a multisectoral approach similar to the one it promoted through its earlier interventions to expand Bengaluru metro and the Delhi-Meerut Regional Rapid Transit System (RRTS) corridor. Along with developing metro infrastructure, this approach extends to transit-oriented development along the metro corridors to enhance access to jobs and socioeconomic services, curb urban sprawling, and reduce dependency on motorized vehicles.

Other projects approved targeted improving road connectivity in Maharashtra, Assam, and Rajasthan to enhance rural communities' access to health and social services; upgrading water supply and sanitation services in the states of Tamil Nadu, Himachal Pradesh, Nagaland, and Tripura; developing infrastructure of industrial estates in Tripura and improving distribution and generation efficiency to ensure Tripura's energy security.

These interventions were complemented by ADB's private sector support to microfinance, electric mobility, water sector, agribusiness sector, crop nutrition, and transport finance.

The intended impact of ADB-supported projects was to spur economic activity, improve the daily lives of people with upgraded basic services in urban and rural areas, enhance connectivity with markets, and improve livelihood opportunities in the aftermath of COVID-19.

8 Beyond the Pandemic: The Enduring ADB-India Partnership

As a long-standing and trusted partner, ADB worked closely with the Government of India to support its pandemic management strategy during different phases and the post-pandemic recovery effort. Moving swiftly, as the situation demanded, ADB provided several targeted interventions to support India during the early stages of the emergency. In doing so, ADB tailored its regular operations and business processes to meet the immediate and emerging requirements of the Government of India.

Notwithstanding the disproportionate effect of the pandemic on poor and vulnerable populations in India during 2020–2022, the overall economy has since largely recovered. Growth is gradually being revitalized and returned to a firmer footing, led by the increased public investment for infrastructure development, private investments, exports, and consumption. India's GDP is projected to grow 6.4% in financial year (FY) 2023 and 6.7% in FY2024.[54]

Going forward, ADB is committed to working with the Government of India to meet the country's aspirations for a fast recovery from the pandemic as well as inclusive and sustainable growth. To achieve this, ADB will support India in strengthening its health care and social protection systems and assist small- and medium-sized enterprises to bounce back from the pandemic. ADB will increase investments in education, finance, and public sector management. Support for industrial corridor development to spur manufacturing and job creation, improve urban livability, skill development, multimodal logistics development, and India's climate-action commitments lie at the core of ADB's India operations over the next 5 years.

The country partnership strategy (CPS) for India, 2023–2027, provides the roadmap for meeting these aspirations and commits ADB to help the country address key challenges in the post-pandemic era (Figure 8.1). The CPS seeks to catalyze robust, climate-resilient, and inclusive private sector-led growth by accelerating structural transformation and job creation, promoting climate-resilient green growth, and deepening social and economic inclusiveness. These strategic objectives are tied to India's national development priorities to be achieved by 2047, when the country marks 100 years of independence.

Through three clearly defined strategic pillars, the CPS addresses to the Government of India's priorities for generating more formal sector jobs, meeting India's climate action commitments, and assisting lower-income states in their development objectives. First, ADB is focused on helping India's structural transformation through the promotion of industrial corridors, multimodal logistics hubs, and urban centers as engines of growth and skill development. Second, it is supporting climate-resilient green growth by strengthening India's energy transition, decarbonization of transport, climate change adaptation, disaster risk management, and circular economy. Third, ADB is supporting India in generating inclusive growth.

---

[54] A financial year in India refers to the period from 1 April to 31 March (e.g., FY2023 = 1 April 2022–31 March 2023); ADB. 2023. India's Economy Grows 6.4% in FY2023. News Release. https://www.adb.org/news/india-economy-grow-6-4-fy2023-rise-6-7-fy2024.

Figure 8.1   The Three Pillars of the Asian Development Bank's India Country Partnership Strategy, 2023–2027

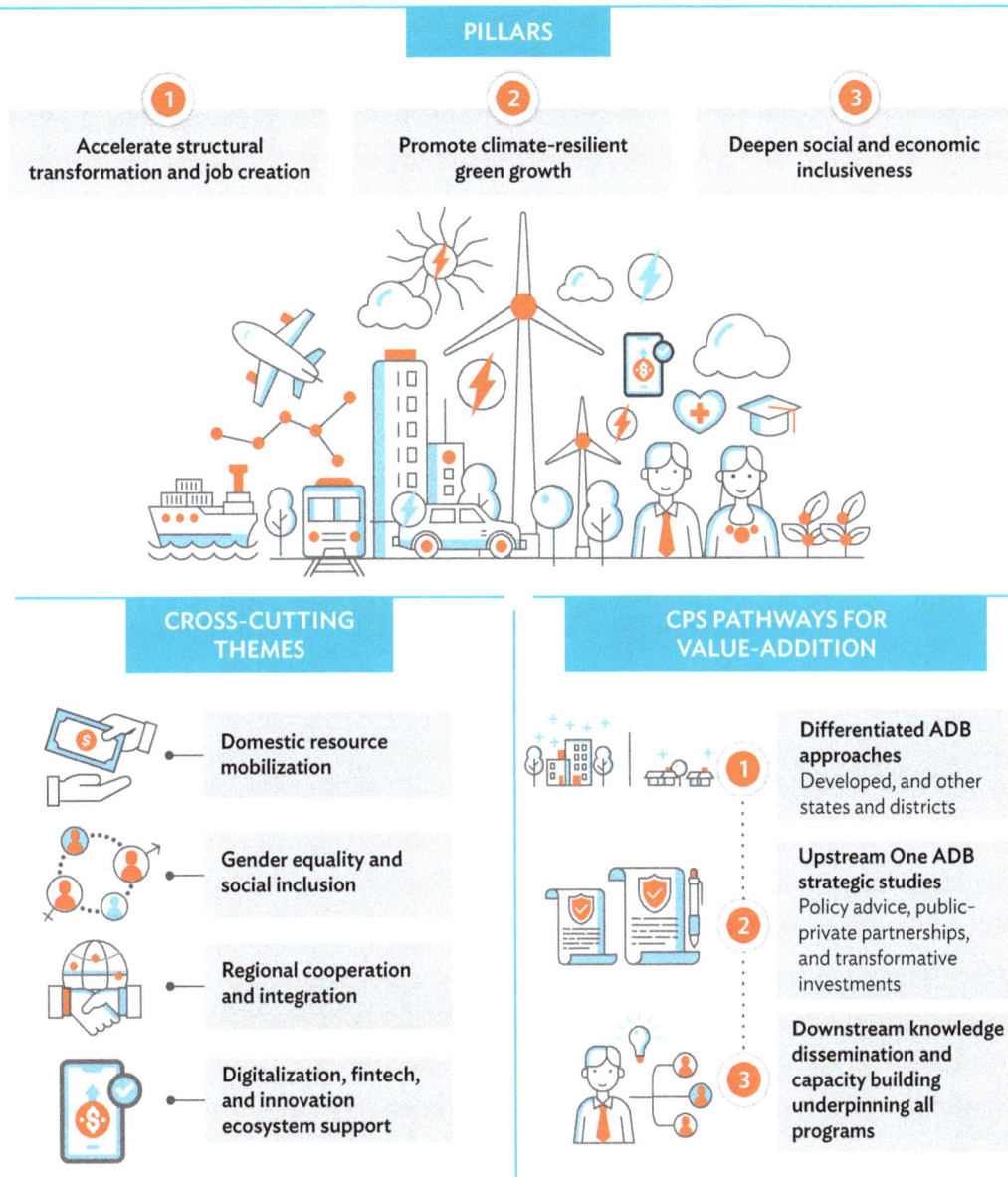

PILLARS

1 Accelerate structural transformation and job creation

2 Promote climate-resilient green growth

3 Deepen social and economic inclusiveness

CROSS-CUTTING THEMES

Domestic resource mobilization

Gender equality and social inclusion

Regional cooperation and integration

Digitalization, fintech, and innovation ecosystem support

CPS PATHWAYS FOR VALUE-ADDITION

1 Differentiated ADB approaches — Developed, and other states and districts

2 Upstream One ADB strategic studies — Policy advice, public-private partnerships, and transformative investments

3 Downstream knowledge dissemination and capacity building underpinning all programs

ADB = Asian Development Bank, CPS = country partnership strategy.
Source: Asian Development Bank.

The CPS applies four cross-cutting themes across all three pillars: domestic resource mobilization (particularly at the municipal level), gender equity and social inclusion, digitalization and support for an innovation ecosystem, and enhanced regional integration. Further, ADB has increased its assistance to improving education, health, and social protection to enhance urban livability and rural development through government initiatives such as AMRUT 2.0, the National Industrial Corridor Development Program, and affordable housing programs for migrant workers and the urban poor. In response to ever-evolving social and economic conditions, ADB will regularly recalibrate its support to India as it moves closer toward developed country status.

Appendixes

Appendix 1

Table A1 Pandemic Response of the Government of India (January–March 2020)

Date	Government Action
Mid-to-late January 2020	• Issued travel advisory for the People's Republic of China • Communicated to Indian states and Union Territories on COVID-19 • Operationalized a 24x7 call center managed by the National Centre for Disease Control
By end of January 2020	• Screened 43,346 international travelers[a] • Operationalized 12 laboratories for testing COVID-19 samples[b]
Early February 2020	• Constituted a Group of Ministers (comprising the ministers of Health, External Affairs, Civil Aviation, Home, and Shipping) to coordinate responses across multiple ministries[c] • Increased the number of countries whose travelers are screened upon arrival • Operationalized screening points at 21 airports, 12 major seaports, and 65 minor seaports and land crossings[d]
By the end of February 2020	• Screened a total of 482,927 travelers from 12 countries[e] • Conducted community surveillance on 23,531 persons across states and Union Territories through the Integrated Diseases Surveillance Programme network[f] • Sent 2,836 samples for testing, of which 2,830 were negative[g]
6 March 2020	• Ministry of Health and Family Welfare and the World Health Organization jointly organized national-level training on COVID-19 for 280[h] health officials from all states, including railways, defense, and paramilitary force hospitals • Rolled out new advisories with the inclusion of several countries whose travelers are required to be put in 14-day quarantine upon arrival

[a] Government of India, Ministry of Health and Family Welfare. 2020. Cabinet Secretary holds high level review on Novel Coronavirus. Press release through Press Information Bureau. 30 January. https://pib.gov.in/Pressreleaseshare.aspx?PRID=1601169.

[b] Note a to Table A1.

[c] Government of India, Ministry of Health and Family Welfare. 2020. High level Group of Ministers constituted on directions of PM, to review management of Novel Coronavirus; First meeting held today. Press release through Press Information Bureau. 3 February. https://pib.gov.in/newsite/PrintRelease.aspx?relid=198889.

[d] Government of India, Ministry of Health and Family Welfare. 2020. Update on COVID-19: Through dedicated and collaborative efforts, we have evacuated 124 persons from Japan and 112 persons from Wuhan: Harsh Vardhan. Press release through Press Information Bureau. 27 February. https://pib.gov.in/PressReleasePage.aspx?PRID=1604508.

[e] Note d to Table A1.

[f] Note d to Table A1.

[g] Note d to Table A1.

[h] Government of India, Ministry of Health and Family Welfare. 2020. Update on COVID-19: Cases and management. Press release through Press Information Bureau. 6 March. https://pib.gov.in/PressReleaseIframePage.aspx?PRID=1605499.

continued on next page

Table A1   *continued*

Date	Government Action
16 March 2020	• Ensured social distancing norms by closing all educational establishments, gyms, museums, cultural and social centers, swimming pools, and theatres[i]
17–18 March 2020	• Prohibited inbound flights operations from member countries of the European Union, the European Free Trade Association, Türkiye, the United Kingdom, Afghanistan, the Philippines, and Malaysia[j]
19 March 2020	• Public transport advised to run with decreased frequency (and later suspended); offices advised to undertake staggered working hours and work-from-home arrangements[k]
20 March 2020	• Barred exports of ventilators, surgical and disposable masks, and textile raw materials used for masks and coveralls[l]
22 March 2020	• Completely suspended inbound international flight operations[m]
24 March 2020	• Completely suspended domestic flight operations[n] • Reported 118 laboratories in the India Council of Medical Research network of COVID-19 testing with a capacity to test 12,000 samples per day[o] • Implemented nationwide lockdown under the National Disaster Management Act, 2005 for an initial period of 21 days
29 March 2020	• Empowered groups[p] led by secretary level officers in 11 key areas to guide the COVID-19 response[q]

[i] Government of India, Ministry of Health and Family Welfare. 2020. High level Group of Ministers reviews current status, and actions for prevention and management of COVID-19. Ministry of Health issues Comprehensive Advisory on Social Distancing. Press release through Press Information Bureau. 16 March. https://pib.gov.in/PressReleaseIframePage.aspx?PRID=1606637.

[j] Government of India, Ministry of Health and Family Welfare. 2020. Note i. to Appendix 1. | Government of India, Ministry of Health and Family Welfare. 2020. Update on COVID-19: Advisories and Guidelines for Containment and Prevention. Press release through Press Information Bureau. 17 March. https://pib.gov.in/PressReleaseIframePage.aspx?PRID=1606838.

[k] Government of India, Ministry of Health and Family Welfare. 2020. High level Group of Ministers reviews current status, and actions for prevention and management of COVID-19. Press release through Press Information Bureau. 19 March. https://pib.gov.in/PressReleaseIframePage.aspx?PRID=1607242.

[l] Government of India, Ministry of Commerce & Industry. 2020. Export of Masks, Ventilators and textile raw material for masks and coveralls prohibited. Press release through Press Information Bureau. 20 March. https://www.pib.gov.in/newsite/PrintRelease.aspx?relid=200505.

[m] Government of India, Ministry of Health and Family Welfare. 2020. Note k. to Appendix 1.

[n] Government of India, Ministry of Civil Aviation. 2020. Operations of domestic schedule commercial airlines to cease operation from the mid night 23.59 IST hours on 24/3/2020. Press release through Press Information Bureau. 23 March. https://pib.gov.in/newsite/PrintRelease.aspx?relid=200619.

[o] Government of India, Ministry of Health and Family Welfare. 2020. UPDATE on COVID-19. Press release through Press Information Bureau. 24 March. https://pib.gov.in/PressReleaseIframePage.aspx?PRID=1607976.

[p] Government of India, Ministry of Home Affairs (MHA). 2020. Released as order No. 40-3/2020-DM-I(A) by MHA. 29 March. https://www.mha.gov.in/sites/default/files/PR_MHAOrderrestrictingmovement_29032020.pdf.

[q] Medical emergency management plan; availability of hospitals, isolation and quarantine facilities, disease surveillance and testing, and critical care training; ensuring availability of essential medical equipment such as personal protective equipment, masks, gloves, and ventilators: production, procurement, import and distribution; augmenting human resources and capacity building; facilitating supply chain and logistics management for availability of necessary items such as food and medicines; coordinating with the private sector, nongovernment organizations and international organizations on response-related activities; economic and welfare measures; information, communication, and public awareness; technology and data management; public grievances and suggestions; strategic issues related to the lockdown.

continued on next page

Table A1   *continued*

Date	Government Action
15 April 2020	• Extended the nationwide lockdown in phases until 31 May (Phase 2: 19 days, Phase 3: 14 days, Phase 4: 14 days)
31 May 2020	• Reported 676[r] labs with testing capacity of approximately 100,000 samples per day at the end of Phase 4 on 31 May • Extended the lockdown into a fifth phase (in containment zones) until 30 June
1 June 2020	• Reported significantly increased daily testing capacity of 100,180 samples[s]

[r]   Indian Council of Medical Research lab report accessed at https://www.icmr.gov.in/pdf/covid/labs/archive/COVID_Testing_Labs_11062020.pdf.

[s]   SARS-CoV-2 (COVID-19) Testing Status accessed at https://www.icmr.gov.in/.

Appendix 2

Table A2   Economic and Demographic Data—Assam

As the largest state in northeastern India, Assam had a population of more than 31 million, or about 2.6% of India's total population,[a] with the share of its under-40 population higher than the national average. Assam reported 13.3% GDP growth in FY2019, exceeding the all-India GDP growth rate that same year. However, it accounted for a mere 1.7% of India's GDP and only 0.1% of national exports in FY2019.[b] Assam's recorded GDP per capita was about two-thirds that of the all-India average in FY2019: India's GDP per capita was ₹142,964 compared to ₹92,533 for Assam.

Assam is trapped in an economic structure in which the primary sector accounts for 29.7% of state GDP and 39.5% of total employment, the secondary sector contributes 23.7% to state GDP and 23.5% to employment, while the tertiary sector's respective shares are 46.6% and 37.1%.[c] Its undiversified small-sized manufacturing sector accounted for a mere 12.3% of GDP in FY2019, compared to 16.1% for India.

FY = financial year, GDP = gross domestic product.

[a]   Government of India, Ministry of Home Affairs, Office of the Registrar General and Census Commissioner of India. 2011. Census of India.

[b]   https://www.adb.org/sites/default/files/linked-documents/53277-002-ea.pdf.

[c]   Government of India, Ministry of Statistics and Programme Implementation. National Accounts Statistics and Periodic Labour Force Survey.

www.ingramcontent.com/pod-product-compliance
Lightning Source LLC
Chambersburg PA
CBHW050050220326
41599CB00045B/7351